THE NATURAL INSOMNIA SOLUTION

How to Fall Asleep, Stay Asleep, Restore Your Health and Regain Your Sanity Without Medication

Dr. Doni Wilson, ND, CPM, CNS

ISBN 13: 978-1791503840

Be sure to get the most out of this book by getting the Sleep Checklist. The steps in the checklist match up with the 12 common causes of sleep issues covered in the book, so you can use the checklist as you read the book, and as a way to get started right away on resetting your sleep pattern.

Download the Sleep Checklist at
DoctorDoni.com/sleepchecklist

And when you do, I'll also send you more support for a good night's sleep.

Dr. Doni

TABLE OF CONTENTS

INTRODUCTION

Looking at Sleep in a New Way

This book examines insomnia – and sleep issues in general – with a perspective different from what most of us have been brought up to believe. And because this perspective is so different, the approaches to restoring good sleep may also be different from what you might have expected.

I am saying this now because I want you to know just what you're getting into. This book has the potential to create major change – not just in your sleep, but in your day-to-day lifestyle, your relationships and the things you value as most important.

Whether you suffer from only occasional wakefulness or you have had ongoing, major sleep issues for many years, it is important to meet this book with an open mind. More than that, you will need to come with a willingness to take a good, honest look at your whole life: the foods you eat, the activities you choose, your environment and your thoughts.

In other words, we will be addressing your **whole health**. Only by looking at 'all of you' will be able to attain lasting improvement in your sleep. This is because the quality of your sleep is a *direct indication* of your health overall. Health issues tend to cause sleep disruption, and sleep disruptions lead to health issues. It is vicious cycle that we can only break by addressing the big picture.

So, this book is not for someone who is looking for a quick fix. While certain nutrients, herbs or dietary changes can surely help with your sleep issues, in the short-term, for *lasting change* to occur, we need to take into account *everything* that influences your sleep – every hormone, every neurotransmitter, every cytokine and even your genes.

Most of all, we need to examine your stress levels.

The reason why we need to look at all of these factors is that insomnia is not just a matter of not being able to fall (or stay) asleep at night, but a *potentially serious health issue caused by stress-related imbalances in the body.*

Modern medical research has shown that such diverse health issues as anxiety, depression, migraines, dementia, diabetes, heart disease and cancer are all caused by a combination of inflammation and stress (emotional, physical and toxic stresses). I believe the same can be said about insomnia. Thus, insomnia can never be truly or simply solved by taking sleep medications, as they do nothing to restore the balance your body needs to have regular and restful sleep. Don't take this to mean that you should stop taking a medication you are currently taking - that is up to you and your doctor to decide. My intention is to point out the goal of this book, which is to address insomnia BEYOND the use of sleep medications.

It's not that I have it out for medications just because I'm a naturopathic doctor. In fact, naturopathic doctors are trained and licensed to *prescribe* medications in certain jurisdictions. It's that I can see, as have many of you, that prescription sleep medications (referred to as Z meds) can have severe consequences on your health.

Research shows that after only 90 days of using prescription sleep medications such as benzodiazepines and diphenhydramine, you *double* your risk of having a car accident the following day, and *triple* your risk of developing Alzheimer's disease. Aside from these shocking statistics, these drugs also have a long list of other potential side effects.

Still, according to a recent Consumer Report, 37% of people who complained of sleep problems at least once per week said they had used an over-the-counter or prescription sleep medication in the previous year. And half of the people who take sleep aids use the drugs in potentially harmful ways. Some take sleep drugs without allowing enough hours to sleep at night; others take them more often or for a longer period of time than recommended. Still others combine these drugs with other medications or supplements.

Apart from prescription medications, it is estimated that 16% of people drink alcohol to help them sleep. Alcohol, a substance known to have negative consequences on health, especially when consumed in large amounts and daily.

Medication or alcohol can never provide a true solution for insomnia. Sure, medication is sometimes necessary for a period of time; but the belief that there is a 'miracle pill' out there that will solve your sleep issues and fill a mysterious void is pure fantasy – one that is likely to drag out the process and increase your health risk by tacking on days, weeks, years of unrestful sleep, creating even more risks to your health and wellbeing.

Fortunately, as I aim to show in this book, there *are* natural solutions you can use to help address those imbalances and reduce the stress within your body, so you can finally get the sleep you need, and eliminate the need for (or dependence) upon medications. But while I can give you all the information you will need to approach your sleep problems in this way:

…THIS APPROACH WILL ONLY WORK IF YOU ARE WILLING TO LOOK AT SLEEP, YOURSELF AND THE WORLD AROUND YOU IN WHAT MIGHT BE A COMPLETELY NEW AND UNFAMILIAR WAY.

Setting Your Health Goal

Before we get started, I encourage you to take a few minutes here and think about (and preferably write down) your health goal.

What is the feeling you want to have when you go to sleep and when you wake in the morning? I understand your goal right now might that is something like "I just want to sleep through the night." But I want you to take it a step further and identify **a vision** of what your life will look and feel like when you sleep through the night. What will that experience be like for you? The more we can help clarify that experience for your mind, the more your mind will help you attain it.

Once you can see this vision, make a post-it note or draw a picture of it, and paste it somewhere you will see it every day – preferably in the morning. This way, just as you would do when exercising a muscle, you can "exercise" the feeling of *experiencing your vision,* and keep it in your daily meditation or focus for the day.

Getting into the right state of being for sleep

I have one more request for you before we can truly dive in to solving your sleep issues: to create a sense of gratefulness and forgiveness within yourself. I know, I know, you may be wondering what the heck this has to do with sleeping. But over the years of working with thousands of patients with all forms of insomnia, I found they shared one thing in common:

THEY FELT ANGRY WITH THEIR BODY FOR NOT SLEEPING!

Feeling angry with your body *will keep you awake at night*. So, if you really want to sleep at night, it's vital to be able to feel grateful for your body, and to *forgive your body* for not sleeping well.

Doing this might feel awkward or absurd at first. I get that you may have never thought of "forgiving your body" before. But try to see your body not as a "thing" outside yourself, but as part of who you are as a sentient *human being*. Because your body is indeed human and not a robot, it is extremely responsive to its environment. Thus, if something in its environment – toxins, emotional stress, inflammation, food sensitivities, etc. – is upsetting it, it simply might *not be able to* sleep well. The only way to stop feeling *angry* with your body is to learn how to see its distress through compassionate, forgiving eyes.

I can understand how infuriating it is to sit awake at night, staring at the ceiling, wishing you could fall to sleep. Trust me, I've been there! But turning that anger at yourself or your body is only going to work against you, and make the problem worse. If you can acknowledge your frustration without blaming or judging your body, I believe you'll find a whole new space within yourself that can help your body *recover* and get back to sleeping...which is what both you and your body really want and need.

Guiding you – and your body – back into balance

The fact that you've not been sleeping well tells me that *your body needs attention*. Knowing *where* it needs attention and *how* to give it that attention it needs is where I step in.

Perhaps you're a mom with young children, or a dad with a lot of responsibility, or not happy in your relationship, or taking care of aging parents, or a business owner.

Or perhaps you are not sleeping enough because you have so many other things to get done. Again, I've been there. In fact I had to lose sleep in order to write this book about how to get good sleep - simply because there were no other hours to get it done.

Here is one of the most important things I remind myself every day - it's NOT that we get nothing done while sleeping. We get a LOT done while we sleep. In fact our bodies do quite a lot of repair and our brain literally cleans out built up proteins WHILE we sleep.

So sleep is essential. And that is why you are reading this book and why I wrote this book. But please don't stress about not sleeping.

Sleep is what happens when we are NOT stressed. If you are under a lot of stress, sleep is one of the first things affected. We've got to break that pattern and get ahead of it.

How do we get you back to sleeping well? There are situations and responsibilities in life that don't just "go away" but there are also ways to support ourselves while under stress so that we can maintain our health and potentially resolve the stress more efficiently because we are well rested.

In fact, my sole aim throughout the rest of this book will be to guide you through that very process.

Okay, I've said what I wanted to say before we started our work together. Now, as soon as you feel you are ready, let's begin.

CHAPTER 1

WHY YOU NEED A GOOD NIGHT'S SLEEP

SLEEP...

It's one of the most natural things in life. It's also one of the most important things we can do for our health. We spend, on average, one-third of our lives asleep. During that time, our hormones are busy at work – healing, growing and restoring the cells in our bodies. Yet research indicates that a large proportion of people get less than seven hours of sleep each night.[1],[2]

Most of us have experienced periods in our lives when insomnia has caused us to feel unwell and function poorly during the day.[3] What you might not realize is your insomnia (or other sleep problems) may be caused by (or be symptoms of) a range of other health conditions.

Chronic lack of sleep makes us vulnerable to infections, metabolic disturbances, inflammation, and oxidative stress. The stress it puts on our bodies has been proven to predispose us to a number of health issues including frequent colds, sinus infections, weight gain, heart disease, depression, dia-

1

betes[4], Alzheimer's[5] and – yes – even *cancer*. That's how important sleep is to a functioning human body.

Poor sleep cannot always be excused away by saying, "I have a lot on my mind." It could be due to a hormone imbalance or food sensitivities, or you might have blood sugar issues or irregularities in your neurotransmitters. Unless you actually KNOW what is causing you to have poor quality sleep, you won't know what to do about it.

Sleep is also influenced by our genetics and exposure to stress starting from a young age. Even with genetic tendencies, we can still improve sleep by using the approaches in this book.

I consider sleep to be one of the "seven essential pillars of total wellness." That's why when I meet with a new patient, one of the first questions I ask is, "How is your sleep?" It is also why I developed an entire naturopathic protocol JUST for sleep issues.

And it's why I have written this book.

What you might be experiencing

Every year, I see hundreds of clients in my private practice. At least 50% of them complain that they have trouble sleeping. While everyone is different, most patients with sleep issues will exhibit one or more of the following symptoms:

- Inability to fall asleep and/or stay asleep at night
- Feeling unrefreshed upon rising in the morning

- Tiredness, drowsiness or feeling the need to take a nap during the day
- Tossing and turning; unable to "switch off" at night
- Recurring headaches
- Frequent infections (including bladder, sinus, etc.)
- Frequent colds or flu
- Food cravings, especially for carbohydrates and caffeine
- Uncontrollable or unexplained weight gain
- Aches and pains (including fibromyalgia or arthritis)
- Anxiety, overwhelm or low mood
- PMS, irritability or a proneness to mood swings
- Brain fog while trying to work
- Difficulty focusing and/or difficulty with memory

If you recognize yourself in any of these symptoms, you've picked up the right book. In this book, you will learn:

- The 12 most common causes for insomnia and poor sleep
- How to determine which of these is causing your sleep problems
- Practical steps to restore your precious sleep – without drugs, alcohol or other "desperate" measures

So this book is more of a workbook. The plan and steps to implement are integrated along the way in each chapter. Then I put it all together in my Sleep Recovery Protocol for you to follow for the greatest likelihood of improved sleep.

At the end of this book, you will also find information about resources to support sleep, including my online programs, consultation packages and health panels, as well as various herbs and supplements recommended within the book. I wanted to ensure these were easy for you to find, so whenever you see a word that is hyperlinked, click it if you would like more information.

Before we begin our journey together, I would like you to set your intention to commit to *applying* some of the information provided within these pages. I also strongly advise you to reach out to a reputable naturopathic doctor to assist you with the suggestions in this book and to help guide you as you make these crucial life changes.

Now, I want you to take a deep breath and shut your eyes…

…and imagine how your world will change when you are getting a good night's sleep every night for the rest of your life. How will you feel in body, mind and spirit?

Take a few moments to relish that image. When it has become vividly imprinted in your heart and mind, turn the page to begin the path back to health, happiness…

…and sanity.

CHAPTER 2

12 Reasons Why You May Not Be Sleeping at Night

In our modern world, so many of us find it difficult to switch off at night and get the vital sleep we need to stay happy and healthy, both in body and mind. Many of us blame our daily woes and overactive brains for those long, restless nights; but the actual reasons for your sleeplessness might have nothing to do with either of these. Even taking genetics into account doesn't always identify a single cause for sleep issues. That's because there can be multiple, often inter-related causes, creating a vicious cycle of sleeplessness and genetic tendencies.

Here are 12 common reasons – some of which you might not have thought of – why you may be having trouble falling (or staying) asleep at night.

REASON 1: Timing

Human beings need between 7.5 and 9 hours of **uninterrupted sleep** every night. This means that even if you get 7.5 hours of sleep, but you wake up during the night, you aren't getting enough. And it's not just about the number of hours you sleep, but WHEN you sleep. Genetics play a role in circadian rhythm and how many hours of sleep are best for you.

In one study, nurses who worked the night shift were at increased risk of gaining weight[6] compared to those who slept between 10 pm and 8 am. Shift work that disrupts your normal pattern of sleep can also increase your cancer risk[7].

REASON 2: Environment

Everything from light exposure to noise, temperature, electronic devices, television viewing[8], allergens, and pets can potentially affect your sleep. In some cases, the environment keeps you awake later, leaving you more tired the next day[9].

In other cases, it may be that you are wakened by a pet, child or noise (a snoring bed partner, for example) and then find it difficult to get back to sleep. Perhaps you can think of ways the environment in your bedroom may be affecting your sleep.

REASON 3: Waking to Use the Bathroom

Known as "nocturia", night time waking to urinate can also be a cause of disrupted sleep. Nocturia can be caused by pregnancy, benign prostatic hypertrophy (BPH), interstitial cystitis (inflammation in the bladder), muscle weakness, side effects from medications, or other triggers. Regardless of the underlying reason, waking up to use the bathroom can lead to ongoing sleep issues, as it reduces your hours of uninterrupted sleep.

REASON 4: Blood Sugar Imbalances

If your blood sugar spikes and then drops again while you are sleeping, it will quite likely wake you up. This can happen when you eat a high carbohydrate snack before bed (even if it's fruit).

If you have insulin resistance or diabetes, or a genetic tendency to elevated blood sugar levels, you are more likely to be woken by blood sugar fluctuations. You are also more likely to develop sleep apnea which is when your breathing in disrupted while sleeping causing decreased oxygen in your blood[10].

REASON 5: Elevated Cortisol

Cortisol should be at its lowest at 10 pm in the evening and remain low until it rises in the morning (peaking at 6 am). With exposure to stress, cortisol, as well as adrenaline, levels can be thrown off track and remain high at night. When that happens, sleep is disrupted and insulin becomes less effective[11], leading to higher blood sugar levels and weight gain. Certain genetic patterns can make elevated cortisol more likely.

REASON 6: Weight Gain

Both elevated blood sugar and cortisol make weight gain more likely. Genetics also play a role. Sleep apnea – which occurs when breathing is blocked during sleep, causing oxygen levels to drop – is much more likely with weight gain.

Both sleep apnea and weight gain increase inflammation and risk of high blood pressure and heart disease[12].

REASON 7: Inflammation and Pain

Obesity leads to inflammation[13] and oxidative stress within the body, both of which are associated with worsening sleep. Inflammation spreads throughout the body and may be felt as pain in your joints, back or nerves (such as with sciatica). This pain can be sufficient to wake you in the middle of the night. Some of us have genetic tendencies to inflammation that make this situation more likely.

REASON 8: Leaky Gut, Gluten and Other Food Sensitivities

Sleep issues are common in patients with celiac disease[14] as well as those with non-celiac gluten sensitivity, even if they are following a gluten-free diet. I find that many patients with multiple food sensitivities and with leaky gut tend not to sleep well, and that when they eliminate foods based on an IgG and IgA food panel, they report improved sleep.

It may seem hard to believe that the gut and brain are so interconnected, but research is now proving the link referred to as the "gut-brain axis[15]." Basically foods, like gluten, cause leaky gut and trigger inflammation, which leads to inflammation throughout the body with the potential to disrupt sleep.

REASON 9: Imbalanced Neurotransmitters

Neurotransmitters – the messengers in the nervous system that determine mood, such as serotonin, dopamine, GABA, and glutamate – can affect sleep when the levels are out of balance.

For example, if levels of serotonin or GABA (which are calming neurotransmitters) are too low, sleep may be interrupted. If dopamine, glutamate and/or adrenaline (which are all stimulating) are too high, again, it will be difficult to sleep soundly. It is also well established that neurotransmitters can be thrown out of balance by inflammation and hormonal changes. Genetics definitely play a role in how you make and process neurotransmitters, potentially increases the risk of imbalance and subsequent sleep issues.

REASON 10: Hormonal Changes, Such as Perimenopause

When ovarian function shifts, the hormones produced by the ovaries (estrogen and progesterone) change or decrease, such as with pregnancy, perimenopause, and post-menopause[16]. Women require the right balance between estrogen and progesterone. If this balance is lost, sleep can be affected. In addition, night sweats associated with hormone changes can also cause night-time waking.

REASON 11: Low Melatonin

Melatonin is a hormone that increases at night (its levels are highest at 10 pm), creating our sleep-wake cycle, or circadian rhythm. It has also been associated with the restoration and repair that occurs in our bodies while we sleep. When melatonin levels are decreased, sleep can be disrupted[17], either by not being able to fall to sleep or by not feeling rested in the morning. This is the same effect that occurs temporarily, with jet lag.

REASON 12: Stress

Stress isn't just "all in our heads." It takes a toll on our bodies, too. When we are stressed by work demands or other difficult situations, sleep problems can result[18]. Sleep issues themselves can become a stress, creating a perpetual pattern of insomnia.

This is true for both adults and children[19], and has been shown to lead to elevated cortisol (see Reason 5) and weight gain, which further disrupts sleep (see Reason 6). Once cortisol is elevated, other hormones become less effective (including insulin and melatonin), leaky gut becomes more likely, as does inflammation and neurotransmitter imbalances.

Ultimately insomnia is both caused by stress and perpetuated by the effects of stress. And stress turns on our genetic tendencies, so if stress itself doesn't disrupt sleep, it may eventually cause a genetic predisposition to health issues that throw off your sleep.

Turning It All Around

I want you to know that sleep issues can be solved, even with genetic tendencies and inevitable stress exposure, and even if you haven't slept well for quite a long time.

Turning around your sleep problems starts by understanding what's causing them. Only then can you know the best course of action to take. Thus, over the next twelve chapters, we will take a detailed look at each of these common reasons for poor sleep, and explore ways you can determine which of these problems might be affecting you (and it could be more than one), and how you can solve them safely, naturally and permanently.

To help you understand these sleep problems more clearly, I will also explain the science behind sleep and these things that impair it. Some of the scientific information might seem complex (or you may feel too tired to process it!), but having at least a basic grasp of it will help when you speak with your doctor or naturopathic doctor about your sleep problems. I also find that the more you understand about your body and how it works, the easier it is for you to find solutions that get you back to sleep.

So take it slowly, and only try to absorb as much as you can at a time. Then, put the book down for the day and come back to it tomorrow. You will find yourself gradually learning the information and starting to form a clearer picture of what you need to do to start sleeping soundly again.

So let's begin.

CHAPTER 3

How TIMING Is Crucial to Restful Sleep

I originally wrote this chapter in the month of November, just after most of the U.S. and many other countries in the northern hemisphere had set their clocks back by one hour. It seemed the perfect opportunity to discuss the timing of sleep. I'm sure many of you will agree that even a shift of just one hour can lead to us feeling tired during the day, finding it hard to concentrate, and then having difficulty falling to sleep at night. This problem is compounded when we take a flight partway around the world, or work late and wake early.

As mentioned in Chapter 1, the human adult needs **between 7.5 and 9 hours of uninterrupted sleep every night.** This figure is based on the time it takes us to go through the sleep cycle and the number of times we can complete the cycle in the course of the night.

If you're a parent, you're probably wondering how many hours of sleep your child or teenager needs every night. Here's a rough guide of how their sleep requirements will change as they grow up:

- 0-3 years old: 10 - 18 hours

- 3-5 years old: 11-13 hours

- 6-13 years: 9-11 hours

- Teens: 8 to 10 hours

During any period of sleep, we go through a 1.5-hour cycle made up of two types (REM and non-REM) and four different stages. If our sleep is interrupted at any point during that cycle, we return to the beginning stage. This means if you wake several times in the night, you may never reach the final stages of deep, restful sleep and will wake feeling tired.

Let's look at thestages of the sleep cycle in more detail.

Sleep Stage 1 (Pre-Sleep)

This stage lasts between 5 and 10 minutes. Your eyes are closed, but you could be easily awakened and are not well rested during this stage.

Sleep Stage 2 (Light Sleep)

In this stage, your heart rate slows and your body temperature decreases as your body prepares for deeper sleep. We spend more time in stage 2 than any other stage of sleep (about 50% of sleep is stage 2).

Sleep Stage 3 (Deep Sleep)

This is when you are deeply asleep. It would be hard for someone to wake you from this stage, and if they did, you would feel a bit disorientated. This is the most restorative sleep for your body, necessary for tissue repair and immune system function.

Sleep Stage 4 (REM Sleep)

The transition from stage 3 (deep sleep) back to stage 2 sleep is called "rapid eye movement" (REM) sleep. During this stage, your heart rate and breathing quicken. It is also when you dream, as your brain becomes more active. During your first sleep cycle of the night, you may only spend 10 minutes in REM sleep. However, this gets longer and longer in subsequent cycles, until you spend up to an hour in REM sleep during the final sleep cycle of the night.

The Whole Cycle

A full sleep cycle includes the time it takes to fall to sleep, move through light sleep into deep sleep and then REM sleep, and return to light sleep. Each cycle lasts around 90 minutes. That means if you sleep for 7.5 hours, you'll get 5 sleep cycles during the night; over 9 hours, you'll have 6 cycles.

If you are wondering how well you're sleeping, you might want to try one of the latest technical ways to measure your sleep. You can use your iPhone or smartphone and a sleep app such as Sleep Cycle, SleepBot, or Sleep by MotionX. You just put your smartphone on your mattress while you sleep (make sure it's plugged in or charged!) and it will monitor your sleep and movements. Another option is to use a health wristband such as Fitbit or the Oura ring that tracks your movement and hours of sleep. Both the apps and devices can also wake you at the perfect time – at the end of a sleep cycle.

Tips for Timing

Below are five tips to help improve the timing of your sleep. Keep in mind these are all important for sleep, but you may find that, though you follow all of these steps to the letter, you still have trouble sleeping. If this is the case, something else might be causing your sleep issues. But before we look at anything else, let's start with the basics and think about at what you can do to improve the quality and length of your sleep.

Timing Tip 1 – Determine Your Best Bedtime

To give yourself the best chance of getting at least 7.5 hours sleep, you need to go to bed at the right time. There's no point expecting 7.5 hours' sleep if you have to be up at 6.30 am but don't go to bed until midnight. So, count backwards from the time you need to get up to determine what time you need to go to bed. For example, if you need to wake up at 6:30 am, you need to *be asleep* by 11 pm. This may mean you need to be *in bed* by 10:30 pm to give yourself time to read or settle down.

Timing Tip 2 – Optimize Your Exposure to Melatonin

Melatonin (the hormone that helps you sleep) is at its highest levels at 10 pm, so to get the most benefit from it, you need to be asleep before then. If you are accustomed to going to bed later than that, this may take a bit of planning. You may need to get into bed by 9:30 pm if you like to read before falling asleep, or you may need to get your evening routine completed earlier than usual.

If you normally stay up much later than 10 pm, you might need to work your way back to a 10 pm bedtime little by little so you don't find yourself staring at the ceiling for long periods of time, waiting to get tired. Our bodies can only adjust the time we go to sleep by 30 to 60 minutes each night, so expect it to take a few days or even a week to change your bedtime. We'll be talking more about melatonin in Chapter 12.

Timing Tip 3 – Minimize Disturbances

As we have seen, if you are awakened during the night, your sleep cycle will be disrupted and you won't get enough deep, restorative sleep. If this is the case, you need to start strategizing ways to prevent that from happening. Is your cat or dog waking you? Is noise waking you up? What steps can you take to minimize these disruptions? Perhaps you need to make some adjustments or communicate with others in your living space to figure out how you can make sure your sleep is uninterrupted.

Timing Tip 4 – Get Comfortable

We will take a detailed look at your sleeping environment in the next chapter, but the first step is to make sure
your bed is comfortable. Do you need a new mattress?
Does your pillow work well for your head and neck? Is
your bedding cozy, clean and hypo-allergenic? Can you
make your sleeping room dark and the right temperature
for you?

Timing Tip 5 – Calm Your Mind

If you find it difficult to switch off when you go to bed
and your mind just keeps going over and over things, you
might find a simple relaxation technique helpful. Referred to
as progressive relaxation, Yoga Nidra or a "body scan," the
process described here has the potential to help get you out
of your thoughts and into sleep.

Think about each of your body parts, starting from your
toes and working up. Breathe in while you wiggle your toes;
breathe out as you release any worries or thoughts. Breathe in
as you gently squeeze the muscles in your legs; breathe out as
you relax your muscles and let go of any tension you are holding on to. Continue this as you work up your body to your
head. If you notice any thoughts, remind yourself that you
can handle them tomorrow (you can even write them on a
notepad to remind you, if that helps). Allow your focus to be
on your dreams.

What If These Steps Don't Work?

While many people find these five simple steps are enough to get their sleep rhythm back on track, many others will continue to experience sleep problems. It is true that your sleeplessness could be the result of hormones, blood sugar fluctuations, neurotransmitter imbalances, inflammation or all of the above. However, it's always wise to consider the simplest explanations before jumping to the conclusion that you have an underlying medical issue.

For that reason, the next thing we'll be looking at is your sleep *environment.*

CHAPTER 4

CREATING A BETTER SLEEP ENVIRONMENT

As mentioned earlier, if you normally get the optimal 7.5 to 9 hours sleep per night, it means you spend almost one-third of every day in bed. By the time you are 75 years old, you will have spent 25 years in your bed. That's more time then we do most anything else!

In spite of this, in today's modern world, too many of us lack the kind of sleep environment that is conducive to high-quality sleep. By the time you land in bed at the end of the day, hoping to get a full night's rest, it's too late to change your mattress and bedding; and although with a busy schedule, it may be the last thing on your list, it is incredibly important to your sleep and your health to make sure your sleeping environment is just right.

If you think something in your sleeping environment may be throwing off your sleep patterns, here are six tips for making your sleeping space optimal for getting the rest you need. It is worth the investment - just as you would invest in a car and home - to be sure your sleep quality and efficiency is as good as it can be.

Environment Tip 1 – A Clean and Comfortable Bed and Bedroom

Making sure you have a good sleeping environment means starting with the most basic ingredient:

YOUR MATTRESS!

If you are sleeping on a synthetic mattress (not organic), you are being exposed to a lot of toxins while you sleep. Memory foam mattresses are filled with four gallons of flame-retardant and covered with stain-resistant chemicals which off-gas (release trapped chemicals) petrochemicals over time. These chemicals go into our bodies and can be measured in urine. Many health issues are associated with the chemicals from mattresses including allergies, migraines, fatigue, pain and arthritis, as well as dementia and cancer.

I found for myself that I was getting headaches, and not just any headaches, but severe abdominal migraines, due to sleeping on a non-organic memory foam mattress. So I went on a mission to find a mattress that didn't make me sick, and could actually benefit my health.

I learned that mattresses with metal springs send electro-magnetic signals that increase inflammation. Add electromagnetic signals from cell phones and routers, and it is enough to fully inhibit signals within your body. Dreaming decreases and brain fog increases.

Then, when you consider dust mites, mold, mildew, bacteria and dander that accumulate in your bedding and bedroom, let alone other compounds in the air from paint, furniture, candles, fragrances, dry cleaning, smoke and exhaust, it can quickly add up to quite a polluted space.

If your mattress is really old or if it is synthetic, it may be time for a new one. If that's the case, I encourage you to consider getting one made from fully organic materials such as natural wood, cotton, rubber and/or wool, which are naturally anti-microbial and dust-mite-proof. Cotton is the best option if you are sensitive to chemicals and odors, and a wool mattress (or topper) makes for soft comfortable support. Be careful because many mattress companies advertise as "organic" and yet use partially synthetic materials without adequate support for your spine.

Optimal spine support comes from sleeping on a bed made with wooden slats that move with your body and allow for an optimal position. Even better is to sleep at a slight incline of 3 to 5 percent in order to optimize lymph flow, detoxification, and blood flow. By sleeping in a bed that allows your body to function at its best while you sleep, you will be adding years to your life by preventing the health issues associated with toxin exposure and cramped body positions. An example bed of this type and quality is a Samina bed, handmade in Germany (check resources section of book).

It's also important to cover your mattress and pillows in barrier cloths, ideally also organic, that will protect you from dust mites. Studies show that mattress and pillow covers help

23

with eczema and other allergic conditions; plus, they protect your bedding from exposure to liquids (like sweat). Sheets, blankets and duvet covers also come in organic, non-toxic materials, and should be washed regularly in hot water (130 degrees Fahrenheit to kill dust mites). Wool has been shown to be a better option than down because wool is lightweight and prevents dust and mold, and it also has a cooling effect that minimizes sweating

Research has also shown that clutter in the bedroom can affect your sleep, so remember to take time each day to put away laundry, unpack your suitcase from a trip (if you haven't already) and organize your things. This way, when you get into bed you're less likely to be thinking of everything that needs to get done.

There is also evidence that some people are sensitive to electricity (EMFs) in the bedroom, so removing electrical devices such as cell phones, computers and the TV could benefit your sleep. You may even want to try turning off your internet router to decrease EMFs further.

Environment Tip 2 – Clean Air

We hear about air pollution all the time, but we don't tend to think about it in our homes. However, the air in our houses and bedrooms is full of tiny particles of dust, dander, mold, viruses and other toxins that can aggravate allergies, irritate our airways and can affect our ability to get a good night's sleep.

An air purifier with a HEPA (High Efficiency Particulate Air) filter can eliminate 99% of dust, dander, mold, smoke, and particles that are 0.3 microns or bigger. Some purifiers can even filter smaller particles (referred to as ultra-fine particles) down to 0.1 microns, such as viruses, car exhaust, and pollutants from industrial plants. You will find a list of suggested air filters in the Third-Party Products and Resources listed at the end of this book.

If you don't want to buy an air filter (or can't afford to), even just opening the window to air out the room on a regular basis can do wonders.

Another option is to get a whole house air filtration system and/or special furnace filters that can remove at least 90% of allergens and particles that are 2 microns or larger. Furnace filters usually need to be changed about every six months, so if your filter hasn't been changed lately, be sure to put it on your "to do" list, and choose a filter that is intended to help with allergies.

Environment Tip 3 – Darkness

Light exposure decreases melatonin production; darkness increases it. Melatonin is the hormone that plays a key role in our circadian rhythm (or body clock). It is responsible for making sure you are awake when you should be (during daylight) and getting you to sleep when you should (at night). It also plays a role in recovery and immune system function.

It is therefore crucial to create an environment that allows your body to produce enough melatonin to ensure you get enough good quality sleep and you get the maximum benefit from it. This means making your sleeping environment as dark as possible. Even lights from a filter or device in your room (the standby light on a TV or the light from your mobile phone), or from a street light outside your window, can be enough to disrupt your circadian rhythm and your sleep, even when your eyes are closed.

Some of my patients tell me they sleep with the TV and/or lights on. They say the light and sound creates a comfort and distraction that allows them to sleep. However, too much light while you sleep can disrupt your circadian rhythm and therefore the quality of your sleep, so it's best to turn off the TV and lights and allow your body to sleep without distraction.

Take notice of any light you may be exposed to while you sleep and find ways to change the situation. Sometimes it can be as easy as putting a darker cover over the window, or covering the lights on any necessary devices in your room (or removing the unnecessary ones). For some, sleep masks can also provide an easy and inexpensive solution.

It's also important to consider light exposure in the hour or two prior to sleep. It is specifically the blue part of light that inhibits melatonin. If you know you'll be working at your computer or in a bright room prior to sleep, you can wear a pair of special blue-light blocking glasses to prevent the light from affecting your sleep. You will find information about these glasses in the Third-Party Products and Resources at the back of this book.

If you work late or have a night shift, you'll want to make sure that your bedroom is dark when you sleep even if you are sleeping during daylight hours.

Melatonin is so important for sleep it has a chapter of it's own later in the book.

Environment Tip 4 – Temperature

Interestingly, our body temperature drops while we sleep, reaching a minimum temperature during the period of the night when we sleep most deeply (about four hours before we wake). To optimize your sleep, you'll want to allow for this drop in temperature by managing the temperature in the room and bed.

The ideal temperature for sleeping is not too cold, but not hot either. A room that is too cold or too hot leads to more wake-ups and less restful sleep. Research indicates that sleeping in a room that is slightly cooler – between 60 and 67 degrees Fahrenheit – makes for deeper sleep, less wakeful-ness, and feeling more refreshed the next day.

Find a temperature that feels comfortable to you and is slightly on the cool side, and consider getting a cooling mat or pad if you need help cooling your body temperature. You will find a few suggestions in the Third-Party Products and Resources at the back of this book.

Environment Tip 5 – Non-Toxic Décor

Paints, floor coverings and curtain fabrics can all contain, or be treated with, chemicals that release toxins into the air. These toxins can have long-term effects on health that impact your ability to sleep well. Fabrics and carpets are also trap dust that can aggravate allergies and affect your sleep.

When you paint your bedroom walls, choose non-toxic VOC-free paints. Remove carpeting in order to reduce dust and toxins and choose wood (with a non-toxic finish) or tile flooring instead. Replace old curtains and shades with untreated wooden blinds or organic fabric shades.

Environment Tip 6 – Shhhh, Quiet

It sounds obvious, but quiet can make all the difference to your sleep, and noise can disrupt your sleep even when everything else is going well. Get to know what works best for you and how likely you are to be woken by night-time noises. In some cases, it's not so much about quiet as it is about consistent sounds, which may even cover up more disruptive noises.

White noise can help you sleep better by providing consistent background noise. You can use a white noise machine, a white noise app on your phone (although then you'll have EMFs exposure), or turn on an air filter or fan. For others, complete quiet is the best option. If this is you, ear plugs may work by blocking out all sound while you sleep. Whichever of these approaches you try, you'll know they are helping because you will sleep through the night with no interruptions and you'll feel more rested when you wake in the morning.

Action Steps

Take a minute now to make notes on what you'd like to do to improve your sleep environment, based on what you have read in this chapter.

Do you need to order a filter, new bedding, an organic mattress or ear plugs? Do you want to get a white noise machine and/or find someone to help you clean up clutter, dust or mold in your room? Even if you start with just one step, little by little you will improve your sleep, as well as your health.

CHAPTER 5

ARE TRIPS TO THE BATHROOM DISRUPTING YOUR SLEEP?

One of the first questions I ask my patients when they come to me with sleep issues is whether they wake regularly to use the bathroom at night. It's such an important issue that doctors have given it a name: *nocturia*. In this chapter, we'll be looking at what causes nocturia, how to avoid it, and what you can do to fall quickly back to sleep once you've relieved yourself.

Men, women and children alike often wake at night needing to use the bathroom. Interestingly, in the past, people slept in two phases, each about four hours long, with an hour or two in between to get up, use the toilet and take care of other activities. But when electric light was created, we started staying up later and, as a consequence, the two sleeping periods became condensed into one.

The body produces less urine at night, so it *is* possible to sleep 6-8 hours without having to urinate. Some people, however, wake up to pee for various reasons that we'll discuss more in this chapter. Keep in mind that it is *completely normal,* and not necessarily a health concern, if you wake once or twice a night to use the bathroom. Nonetheless, waking can interrupt your sleep cycle, so if you can prevent it, that would be a good thing.

What Causes Me to Wake Up to Pee?

If you find you are waking more often than every 3 hours, it is important that you see your doctor or urologist to rule other other possible causes.

For both sexes, the most common cause of newly developed frequent urination is a bladder infection, which usually causes pain and a fever, so if that is the case, definitely go to a medical center right away to be evaluated.

Frequent urination can also be a result of inflammation in the bladder (known as interstitial cystitis), and in that case, you would likely experience frequent urination throughout the day as well.

For men, waking to urinate can be a sign of an enlarged prostate. For women, it can be due to menopausal symptoms (which we'll discuss more in a later chapter), or something pressing on the bladder (such as a fibroid , for pregnant women, a baby, or a prolapse of the bladder or uterus). All of these potential causes require attention by a doctor or urologist, so best to make an appointment to find out.

Waking to pee can also happen if you have diabetes, heart disease or kidney disease. Blood work will be able to show if any of these are the case.

There are natural solutions that help with all of these issues, so it's best to find out the cause so it can be addressed. Once you sort out the root of this problem, you will enjoy improved sleep, as well.

What You Can Do to Prevent Night-Time Wake-Ups

In many cases, it's not a full bladder that causes you to wake, but some other disturbance (such as a noise, movement, temperature change, night sweat or pain). Once awake, you feel the need to pee and can be left wondering what came first, waking up or needing to go to the bathroom.

Regardless of what woke you, the key is to be able to fall back to sleep again. Once you need to pee, it's hard to ignore. So what can you do to avoid it in the first place?

- Decrease your fluid intake 2-3 hours prior to going to sleep.

- Avoid drinking fluids that contain caffeine (such as tea, coffee or soda) or alcohol within 6 hours of bedtime. These are *diuretics* and increase your need to pee.

- Use the bathroom right before you jump into bed.

- Do Kegel exercises to strengthen your pelvic floor muscles. This will help increase the amount of time between feeling you need to urinate and actually having to go.

Your pelvic muscles wrap around the bladder. Like any muscle, if you don't use them, they will become weak. Fortunately, it doesn't take a lot of exercise to get them to wake up and respond.

At first, you can just practice squeezing your pelvic muscles and holding them for a count of 5, then release. Think of an elevator: first, squeeze to the first floor. Then try squeezing a little tighter, as if to the second floor and then the third. Keep increasing the tightness and the length you hold the pose. When you can't hold it anymore, release slowly instead of all at once. Repeat that 2-3 times every day. Within a week, you will already see a difference.

Strengthening the pelvic muscles helps to hold up your bladder more, which means it will hold more urine. This means you won't need to go to the bathroom as frequently. If your pelvic muscles are already strong, you don't need to do these exercises.

Once you're awake, if you decide you really do need to pee, it can also create further problems. When you stumble to the bathroom, turn on the lights, pee, and deal with whatever else may catch your attention, it can be so stimulating that you become too awake to go right back to sleep. So what can you do to be sure that you get back to sleep quickly?

- Keep the lights off or as low as possible (as long as you won't trip on your way to/from bed).

- Don't talk or engage in any other activities.

- Try to not let your mind start to think or work. Just focus on getting straight back to bed.

Addressing Nocturia is Important

As mentioned, getting up to pee at night is normal and not necessarily caused by an underlying health issue. Still, we also know you need 7-9 hours of uninterrupted sleep each night to get the maximum benefits for our immune system, metabolism, etc. Thus, if frequent peeing is disrupting your sleep every night, it really is worth taking the simple measures suggested in this chapter, to minimize the chance of nocturia compromising your overall health.

If these measures make no improvement to your nightly wakings, I encourage you to contact your physician or naturopathic doctor to be tested for the possible causes of nocturia we discussed so that you can address it effectively.

CHAPTER 6

How Blood Sugar Levels Affect Your Sleep

In this chapter, we'll focus on blood sugar and how eating too much of the wrong things can pull us into a vicious cycle of over-eating and blood sugar fluctuations that have a serious impact on our ability to sleep.

Have you ever noticed you feel sleepy after a large meal? That sleepiness is due to a rise in your blood sugar levels as the carbs from your meal make their way into your blood stream.

Then the next day you might notice you feel hungrier or you crave sweets. This is because once your blood sugar rises (the technical term for this is *hyperglycemia*) for even just one meal, it will always be followed by a dip in blood sugar (*hypoglycemia*) a few hours later. This dip makes you to want to eat more and repeat the pattern of eating a large amount of carbohydrates.

As you might imagine, once this pattern starts, it's difficult to stop. The more often you consume large meals, the more likely your body is to send the signals that lead you to have another large meal. This is because a rise in blood sugar is followed by a rise in insulin, the hormone that causes the sugar to move into your cells to be used to make energy. Then, when your blood sugar is low again, you are likely to crave **more** sugar and carbs, and in some cases feel tired, irritable, nauseous and even dizzy if you don't eat carbs right away.

This pattern not only throws off your energy, mood and focus during the day, but it can lead to weight gain and disrupt your sleep. This is because any time your insulin function is unable to keep up with the amount of sugar in your blood, the sugar is instead converted into body fat, so you gain weight. Finally, weight gain is associated with sleep apnea and diabetes, which both disrupt sleep, thus creating a vicious cycle of disrupted sleep and weight gain.

SIDENOTE: You might also be surprised to learn that sugar – not fat – increases cholesterol! You can find the link to an article about this, along with many other articles, in the Additional Reading appendix at the end of this book.

So let's take a step-by-step look at how imbalanced blood sugar can disrupt your sleep.

Blood Sugar – Stage 1

Eating sugar or carbs first boosts your blood sugar, giving you a burst of energy that could cause you to stay up later than you'd like, especially if you eat these foods too close to bedtime.

Blood Sugar – Stage 2

As insulin moves the sugar out of your blood and into your cells, you experience the inevitable drop in blood sugar, causing you to feel sleepy and maybe even fall asleep. Good news, right? Wrong!

Blood Sugar – Stage 3

This dip in your blood sugar triggers a stress response in your body, causing both cortisol and adrenaline levels to increase, which could wake you up again! I'll be talking about the role cortisol plays in sleep in Chapter 7. For now, just imagine how you might feel if your body experiences a stress response due to low blood sugar while you are trying to sleep. It is quite likely you'll wake up; you may feel the need to go to the bathroom; and because your body has finished turning that sugar into energy, it now wants more, so you actually feel hungry again, causing you to wake for a midnight snack.

Thus, if you eat a large meal in the evening (or even just a high-carbohydrate snack), you may wake up a few hours after you've gone to sleep due to dropping blood sugar levels. In fact, it's not just the evening meal that can cause these issues. Your blood sugar balance throughout the day influences your blood sugar levels through the night.

If there are peaks and valleys during the day due to high-carb or high-sugar foods (a muffin or piece of cake, for example) or beverages (a coffee drink, soda or juice), or even long hours without eating at all (during which time your sugar levels will fall), then you are more likely to wake at night from the continuation of this pattern.

How to Know What is Happening with Your Blood Sugar

Start by having fasting glucose checked in regular blood work. That means having your blood draw in the morning, before you eat (do drink water). But in my opinion, that is not enough information. I recommend also checking hemoglobin A1c (does not need to be fasting) which indicates your average blood sugar level over three months. If the average is above 5.6, then we know you are having periods of time when your blood sugar is too high.

Elevated hemoglobin A1c (HgbA1c) can be due to consuming too many carbs (and sugar) at one sitting. It can also be due to having elevated cortisol levels, being stressed and not getting good sleep. So we need to get ahead of this right away. Not only does elevated blood sugar lead to diabetes, weight gain and high cholesterol; it also leads to fatty liver, and increased risk of dementia and cancer.

That's why I feel that keeping your blood sugar stable is important ***even if you are not diabetic*** and your blood tests show a normal blood sugar. It's best to start implementing changes to your diet now rather than later, because if this pattern continues unaddressed, it can lead to further issues down the line.

When insulin is responding in high amounts day after day, year after year, because of high-carbohydrate meals and imbalanced blood sugar levels, your cells stop responding to the insulin efficiently (known as insulin resistance or metabolic syndrome) and/or your insulin level can drop permanently (also known as diabetes).

Insulin can be measured in blood work, and is usually tested when fasting (in the morning) along with glucose. If your insulin levels are way up high, you know your pancreas is working overtime to try to keep up the amount of carbohydrates coming through.

This means your blood sugar levels stay high, which can also cause you to feel sleepy after eating carbs because you don't have enough insulin to transport the sugar from your blood into your cells where it can be turned into energy. When it gets to that point, it's even more important to take steps to keep your blood sugar balanced in order to improve your sleep.

How to Keep Your Blood Sugar Stable

The best way to avoid this dangerous pattern is to follow these simple guidelines:

- **Choose protein every time you eat**, along with high-fiber carbs and healthy fats. This can be plant or animal protein, depending on your preferences. Choosing a protein shake as your first meal in the morning, or for a meal later in the day, is a great way to ensure you are getting protein instead of a high-carb breakfast or snack. Learn more about protein shakes I recommend in my article "Protein Powder: A Beginner's Guide" and in the Resources section of this book.

- **Minimize or avoid sugars.** You can find a list of sugars (including many sugars "in disguise") in my article "The Sugar Challenge", which you'll find in the Additional Reading section at the back of this book. Stevia is from a plant and doesn't affect your blood sugar or insulin levels, so it is okay to use. Artificial sweeteners, however, are filled with toxic substances that lead to more trouble.

- **Eat "half-size" meals** so your blood sugar doesn't go so high. Essentially I'm saying to eat less. Even if you start by taking fewer bites each meal, and save that extra food for later. By decreasing the quantity of food in general and specifically the carbohydrates in a single sitting, you'll be stabilizing your blood sugar levels overall, day and night.

- **Eat every 2-4 hours** (depending on your body's needs) during the day so your blood sugar doesn't go too low. If your blood sugar drops quickly, you may need to eat every couple hours. This is a common symptom of adrenal distress (which we'll discuss more soon). If instead you feel bloated if you eat too often, then for you, waiting at least 4 hours between meals may be a better way to go (and again, eat less at a time so you are able to digest the food instead of overfeeding bacteria in your intestines).

- Be sure to have your last meal/food at least 2 hours before bed. Eating too close to bedtime can disrupt your blood sugar levels and increase risk of other health issues. In particular, avoid eating sugar or high-carb foods, especially within 2 hours of bedtime.

The bottom line is:

YOUR BODY DOESN'T REGULATE YOUR BLOOD SUGAR LEVELS – YOU DO!

Your body responds to increasing or decreasing blood sugar levels with hormones that attempt to keep the level steady. If those hormones can't keep up with your eating patterns, they are no longer able to manage the fluctuating blood sugar levels.

So, it's clear that your decisions about what and when to eat have a huge part to play in regulating your blood sugar levels; if you feed your body in a way that keeps your blood sugar levels balanced, you will prevent diabetes and ensure a good night's sleep. This is true even if you have a genetic tendency to blood sugar issues.

Nutrients and Herbs to Help

Chromium is a nutrient that is known to improve insulin function, making it easier for your body to prevent high blood sugar. You can take chromium alone or in a combination product such as Metabolic Xtra. https://www.drdonistore.com/Metabolic-Xtra-90-capsules_p_263.html

Berberine is a substance in several herbs, including goldenseal, and studies show that it not only improves insulin function and drops blood sugar levels, but also effectively helps with diabetes and other conditions associated with high blood sugar (PCOS and dementia). Find it in Metabolic Xtra as well.

Alpha lipoic acid is an anti-oxidant known to help manage blood sugar levels.

Cinnamon, yep the cinnamon we think of as a spice, has been shown to help improve insulin function.

Importance of Balanced Blood Sugar:

Put simply, the more balanced your blood sugar is during the day, the better you will sleep at night. The better you sleep, the less likely it is that you will gain weight, develop diabetes, or any of the other health issues associated with a lack of sleep. If you think this may be what is disrupting your sleep, or if you need more help balancing your blood sugar, be sure to bring this up with your naturopathic doctor.

Keep in mind that stress – both emotional and physical – can amplify an imbalanced blood sugar issue. This is because when cortisol (the stress hormone) is elevated, your blood sugar levels will be even higher – and high blood sugar levels increase your cortisol.

The only way to break this vicious cycle is to get ahead of it by following the tips discussed in this chapter. You may also need to use nutrients and herbs to decrease your cortisol level, as well as exercise and other activities…

…which leads us nicely to Chapter 7, where we will examine cortisol in detail.

CHAPTER 7

How Cortisol Affects Your Sleep

I've mentioned cortisol many times throughout this book, but now it's time to look at it more closely. Cortisol is our primary stress hormone and is produced by the adrenal glands. When a stress response is triggered in the brain, a hormone called adrenocorticotropic hormone (ACTH) signals to the adrenals to make (more of) both cortisol and adrenaline. This stress response system is referred to as the HPA axis (hypothalamic-pituitary-adrenal axis).

Interestingly, cortisol production is both triggered by stress AND produced by our bodies as a *protection* against stress. That means cortisol itself is not a bad thing. But when our bodies produce too much or too little of it at certain times of day, due to ongoing stressors in our lives, it can interfere with our health – and our sleep.

We each have a genetically and epigenetically determined response to stress. I think of your stress response to be as unique as your finger print. We want to find out about your response to stress and how to support it to be as optimal as possible.

What *Should* My Cortisol Levels Be Doing?

Ideally, we don't want our cortisol to be low all day long. In the morning we want cortisol levels to be high, waking us up and giving us the energy to get through the day. Cortisol production should decrease gradually throughout the course of the day, until it reaches its lowest levels late in the evening when we are ready for bed. A good night's sleep requires cortisol to be low and stay low for many hours, until it gradually builds back up to wake us again the next morning.

However, if our stress response is triggered, it can mean that cortisol levels will not decrease in the evening and cortisol production will not shut off at night. If this becomes a chronic situation, it can lead to real issues. In my e-book Stress Remedies, I describe this scenario like this:

> *In a healthy body, the stress response turns on...and then off, allowing the relaxation response to take over. You work hard during the day, and then you rest in the evening. You gear up for a sudden challenge, and then you let go of the tension and return to a relaxed state.*

> *In this balanced state, stress is tolerable, even enjoyable. At worst, life is full of manageable crises that are laid to rest at the end of each day. At best, life is full of exhilarating challenges that bring out your best, leaving you satisfied and fulfilled.*

For many of us, though, the balance has tipped. We can begin to feel as though our stress response is permanently on, with not nearly enough relaxation to balance things out.

In this situation (when cortisol remains elevated), your body receives an energizing signal that makes it difficult to relax and nod off to dreamland. Instead, you are likely to find yourself buzzing around your home, getting lots done, until you realize morning is growing nearer.

Sometimes you'll be aware that you're stressed and your cortisol is elevated, such as prior to a big event or when you have lots to do. Other times, you might not be able to tell your body is stressed, perhaps in response to a past stress or from a physical source of stress within your body (such as leaky gut or inflammation), and is simply unable to turn off the cortisol stress response.

When our stress response is triggered too frequently, it is less able to turn off and therefore more likely to get stuck in an imbalanced state.

Why Is High Cortisol Such a Problem?

It's one thing to understand that a stress response and elevated cortisol could be keeping you awake, but I want to take it a step further. This excerpt from Stress Remedies explains why elevated cortisol and disrupted sleep lead to a vicious cycle of sleep issues and health concerns.

49

Cortisol is so tremendously important in our health and wellbeing that I consider it the "x factor" underlying just about every health problem we face. When our cortisol levels are optimal, we feel terrific. When our cortisol levels are off, we feel anxious and unsettled; fatigued and unmotivated; or, sometimes, both.

After all, stress is the primary condition of life, and cortisol is how we experience stress. Whether we feel exhilarated, thrilled and energized, or listless, jumpy and depressed, cortisol is likely at the root of our experience.

Cortisol has a profound effect on our entire biology. It affects our endocrine system, which produces all our hormones, including thyroid hormone (which regulates metabolism), insulin (which regulates blood sugar) and our sex hormones (estrogen, progesterone and testosterone, which regulate sexual function, menstrual cycles and menopause).

Cortisol has a profound effect on our digestion and our immune system. It also affects our neurotransmitters, the brain chemicals that determine energy, mood, mental clarity, focus and sleep.

Cortisol cues our body to hold onto body fat, so it plays a huge role in weight gain. It is a major contributor to anxiety and depression. When our cortisol levels are optimal, we feel mentally sharp, clear and motivated. When our cortisol levels are off, we tend to feel foggy, listless and fatigued. Cortisol also affects our blood pressure and circulation; our lungs, muscles and bones; and even our skin and hair.

As a practitioner, my first step in almost every situation is to measure my patient's cortisol levels. Almost always, if someone is having health problems, their cortisol levels are out of balance. Until we can restore optimal cortisol levels, my patient's health problems will continue. And when cortisol levels return to optimal, good health will surely follow.

Once cortisol is elevated at night, sleep deprivation is the least of your concerns because the more nights that go by with cortisol high instead of low, the more likely you are to develop digestive issues (such as leaky gut), hormone imbalances, high blood sugar, weight gain, mood changes and/or issues related to your immune system (allergies, autoimmunity, infections and/or cancer).

This is why keeping your cortisol on track is so darn important! And that's why we are going to cover each of those scenarios in the upcoming chapters.

Should I Check my Cortisol Levels?

Yes! I feel that everyone should know their cortisol levels. It is essentially the best "stress test" to know how your body is being effected by and responding to stress. Then, with the information, you have the power to support your body exactly how it needs in order to optimize your cortisol, which has a huge and dramatic influence on the rest of your health and sleep.

If you recently experienced a stressful time in your life that could have thrown off your healthy cortisol curve, it is even more important to have your cortisol levels checked (or rechecked). Not just in a morning blood draw – which would only show your cortisol level at that time of day. Your naturopathic doctor will need to see at least four cortisol levels, starting from the morning, through mid-day, evening and bedtime. And if you are waking in the night, check your cortisol then, as well.

The most effective way to do this is by doing a saliva or urine panel that includes collecting samples at four times throughout the day (and night). The labs that offer these panels will then make a graph to show exactly what your cortisol is up to.

Is it high in the morning and low at night? Spiking in the middle of the night and waking you up?

Adrenaline is Involved as Well

While I've focused mainly on cortisol, our other stress hormone, adrenaline, plays just as big a part in these same areas. Too much or too little of it can really knock us off balance.

For example, when adrenaline is elevated, you are more likely to feel anxious and have difficulty sleeping. When adrenaline is depleted, you are likely to feel tired and have "brain fog". Chronic lack of sleep, low energy, and impaired mental clarity increase our overall stress levels, creating a vicious cycle of stress in our bodies.

What many people don't know is that long-term exposure to stress – even the stress of not sleeping – can actually cause cortisol and adrenaline levels to become too high or too low at various times of day, which can give rise to many other health issues. This is what I refer to as adrenal distress because both cortisol and adrenaline are produced by the adrenal glands.

If we get to this point, our bodies (and brains) will find it difficult to cope with even small, normal daily stressors. Stress will start to cause oxidation in the body (also called "oxidative stress"), which damages cells in the body, skin, and brain, and ultimately causes aging.

Getting Your Cortisol And Adrenaline Tested

If you'd like to get started by having your cortisol and adrenaline levels tested, you can ask your naturopathic doctor to run the test for you. This is a saliva or urine panel that shows your cortisol levels at four different times of day, and a urine test for adrenaline. You can do this test in the comfort of your own home and send your sample to the lab through the mail.

Even better is a dried urine panel that will measure both free cortisol and free cortisone, so we can get a sense of how your body is converting and storing cortisol as well. Find more about the health panels I recommend in the Resources section of this book.

Please note that most mainstream medical doctors are NOT likely to order this test for you.

When your results come in, you'll find out if your cortisol and adrenaline needs to be addressed. Better to do the test than to guess. That way, you can be most efficient with choosing the right herbs and nutrients and the right time of day to take them.

Remember: cortisol affects your blood sugar levels, so when your cortisol is elevated, it's more likely that your blood sugar will be up, too. You may need to address both issues to get the best results. The same goes for food sensitivities; if you are sensitive to gluten and still eating gluten, you are likely to trigger a cortisol response. That elevated cortisol can disrupt your sleep as well as your digestion, furthering the vicious cycle of unwellness.

Restoring Optimal Adrenal Function

For all the reasons I've mentioned in this chapter, adrenal gland function is often in need of attention when you haven't been getting good sleep for a period of time.

In fact, in a person with insomnia, it is quite common to find high cortisol at night, along with low cortisol and adrenaline levels in the morning, when they should be higher than at other times of day. When this happens, you are likely to feel increasingly tired throughout the day.

When I work with patients, I recommend nutrients and herbs to help the adrenal glands recover, to decrease cortisol and adrenaline at night, and to restore healthy cortisol production in the morning, when you want it to be higher and giving you energy for the day.

It is important to choose the right herbs and nutrients for you based on your current cortisol and adrenaline levels, so be sure to have your levels tested before taking herbs and nutrients to be sure you are choosing the correct approach for your body.

I've listed herbs, nutrients and supplements I frequently recommend (you can find links to purchase these online at the back of this book) so you can get a sense of the options.

Nutrients and herbs that can help decrease cortisol include:

Phosphatidylserine is a nutrient known to help decrease the production of cortisol and reset the HPA axis. Take it in the evening to decrease cortisol before sleep. Find it in products by itself, such as in PS Plus, or in combination with herbs that also decrease cortisol, such as Banaba leaf, which can be found in a combination product called Calm CP.

Magnolia root and Ziziphus are two other helps that decrease cortisol. They can be found in a combination product called Seditol. Ashwaganda also decreases cortisol and can be taken alone or in combination with Phosphatidylserine and several other herbs and nutrients that support sleep, such as in **Dr. Doni's Stress Support.**

Hemp oil and cannabinoids in general (without THC) have been shown to help prevent a rise in cortisol when exposed to stress. They are thought to assist with stress recovery and calming the nervous system, which can help with sleep and anxiety. Many hemp oil and cannabinoid products are available in liquid, capsule and topical forms. I recommend starting with a low dose, during the day so you can see how your body responds, and then you can modify the dose and shift it to bedtime for optimal results. Refer to the Resources section of the book for details.

You would take these products in the evening and/or at the time of day when your cortisol and adrenaline are too high to help decrease the levels.

Nutrients and herbs to help lower adrenaline levels and help with sleep:

Magnesium is often depleted when we are exposed to high amounts of stress. Taking magnesium supplements, especially in the form of magnesium glycinate or threonate (versus citrate and oxide) can help calm your nervous system by aiding in processing adrenaline and relaxing your muscles. Another product I often recommend is called Magnesium Plus, which contains both magnesium and vitamin B6.

Vitamin B6 (also known as P5P in the active form) can also be calming because it helps your body to process (and reduce excess amounts of) adrenaline and to support serotonin levels. Again, I recommend the product Magnesium Plus, which contains both magnesium and vitamin B6.

Dr. Doni's Stress Support formula contains both magnesium and vitamin B6, along with herbs and nutrients that support sleep and stress reduction.

Herbs and nutrients that support adrenal gland recovery, as well as healthy cortisol and adrenaline production during the day:

Remember, you would take these formulas when you need and want to increase your cortisol and adrenaline level during the daytime. If you take them at night, or if you take them before you've supported the calming part of your nervous system (covered in chapter 11), then you might experience a boost of energy that could disrupt your sleep. If ever you feel overstimulated, decrease the dose or stop and consider whether you need more calming first.

Dr. Doni's Adrenal Support: Contains tyrosine to support adrenaline, plus herbs and nutrients to support adrenal function and cortisol production, such as vitamin C, pantothenic acid, Eleutherococcus and Glycyrrhiza (herbal licorice).

Adrenal Response: A combination of vitamin C, pantothenate, magnesium, ashwagandha, L-serine, rhodiola extract, holy basil (tulsi) leaf, Cordyceps mushroom mycelia, Reishi mushroom, organic astragulus root, Schizandra, and other active ingredients.

Adrenal SAP licorice-free: A combination of vitamins C, B6 and B5, plus magnesium, zinc, ashwagandha, holy basil (tulsi), Panax ginseng, Siberian ginseng, Schizandra, and astralagus.

Adrecor: Contains the B vitamins, plus vitamin C, tyrosine, and herbs such as Rhodiola and green tea. These have all been shown to restore healthy adrenal function.

Adrecor with Licorice: In addition to the standard Adrecor formula, this product contains licorice extract, which is known to significantly support cortisol levels.

Adrecor with SAMe: In additional to the standard Adrecor formula, this product contains SAMe, which helps with the conversion from norepinephrine to epinephrine, resulting in healthier adrenaline levels, sleep and energy levels.

What You Can Do to Keep Cortisol Optimal

This excerpt from Stress Remedies describes five things you can do to help yourself, whether your cortisol levels are imbalanced or not:

Eat according to your physiology. A key aspect of minimizing the stress on your system is to eat in a way that fits your physiology. The least stressful and most supportive way to nourish yourself is to eat four to six small "half-meals" each day, with each small meal including the correct balance of proteins (30-40%), carbs (30-40%), and healthy fats (20-30%).

Drink plenty of filtered water. *To find the amount you need, divide your body weight in half. That's how many ounces of water you need to drink throughout the day, even if you don't "feel thirsty." You need even more if you are drinking caffeinated beverages, if you are engaged in vigorous physical activity, or if you are in a hot climate. Your thirst monitors don't really reflect your body's need for water, yet when your body becomes even slightly dehydrated, your stress response begins.*

Get 7.5-9 hours of refreshing sleep each night. *We all need sleep—and we need it even more if our waking hours have been full of stressful challenges. Even when we experience these challenges as positive—a new romantic interest, an exciting project at work, a vacation full of thrilling adventures—our body needs time to relax and recover from the demands of the day.*

Implement *Stress Remedies* daily. *There are many activities that have been shown to help our bodies shift out of a stress response, including mindfulness, meditation, yoga, deep breathing, taking a walk, walking your dog, enjoying nature, listening to music, talking* *with a friend, journaling, drinking a cup of tea, and even eating a bite of chocolate. Choose your favorites on a daily basis.*

Exercise at least 15 minutes a day, 3-5 days a week. *Your body was born to move, and when it doesn't get that opportunity, you will find it very difficult to maintain optimal health. Of course, exercise itself is a form of stress—a physical challenge to your body—but paradoxically, it also helps to release stress. A number of studies have shown that regular exercise is associated with decreased anxiety and depression, as well as heart disease, diabetes and cancer.*

In my book - A Guide to Adrenal Recovery - I discuss these daily care essentials that have all been shown to help our bodies recover from stress and become resilient to stress. I organize them with the acronym CARE:

C = CLEAN EATING

A = ADEQUATE SLEEP

R = REDUCE STRESS

E = EXERCISE

The simple strategies in this CARE formula can help you recover from adrenal distress, and prevent it from recurring in the future. Helping you to implement CARE is an essential part of my 7-day Stress Reset, which is an online video and email series, and the Stress Remedy 21-day program (find out more in the Resources at the end of this book).

Attaining and maintaining an optimal cortisol level means you'll probably sleep better. That's why one of the best things you can do for your overall health and wellbeing is re-balance your stress response and cortisol levels. I really cannot "stress" this enough!

Which is why I wrote an entire book on the subject, The Stress Remedy and have created a online course to help you implement, called the Stress Warrior Course.

CHAPTER 8:

How Sleep Apnea and Weight Gain Are Related

In this chapter, we will examine how weight gain and sleep apnea (when you stop breathing for brief periods of time while sleeping) may be affecting your sleep. We'll also look at how getting enough sleep can actually help you *lose* weight, along with natural ways to prevent weight gain and plan for weight loss.

Why Insomnia Makes Us Fat

Studies reveal that when we don't sleep, our hormones become imbalanced, specifically the hormones that manage hunger, appetite (leptin and ghrelin) and blood sugar (insulin) [20].

This means that when you don't get enough sleep you are more likely to feel hungry, which leads you to eat more (especially filling carbohydrates). Because your insulin levels are disrupted and therefore less able to manage the extra carbs and resulting sugars, you are more likely to gain weight – which, in turn, makes inflammation and diabetes more likely[21, 22].

Cortisol, which we looked at in the previous chapter, is another key hormone that makes weight gain more likely if you don't sleep. Cortisol levels are elevated at night in people who don't sleep. That increase is associated with *decreased insulin function* and *increased weight gain*[23].

So, insomnia leads to weight gain, but at the same time weight gain makes it harder to get a good night's sleep. Additionally, weight gain is associated with sleep apnea, which, if untreated, increases your risk of heart disease, diabetes, depression and headaches. Not only that, but sleep apnea also leads to weight gain[24].

It truly is a vicious cycle!

The good news is that when you break this cycle, there is the potential for profound improvements in your health, as well as for slimming your waistline. In fact:

Getting good sleep may be the best non-diet method for losing weight there is.

So in the interests of improving your sleep (and your waistline), let's first look more closely at sleep apnea and how to address it, before tackling weight gain.

Understanding Sleep Apnea

While you might thing one would notice sleep apnea (essentially not breathing for 10-20 seconds, sometimes hundreds of times a night), it's not uncommon for a person to be unaware it's happening.

For some, it occurs when the throat is blocked by extra tissue caused by too much weight (obstructive sleep apnea). For others, it is due to a signaling issue from the brain. Either way, sleep apnea disrupts your healthy sleep cycle, which means you'll benefit less from sleep.

The best way to find out if you have sleep apnea is to have a sleep study at a specialty sleep clinic. They will be able to track your oxygen levels, sleep cycles and wake-up times, among other things, and tell you whether you are experiencing sleep apnea.

You should request a sleep study if:

- You feel unrested when you wake in the morning and/or fatigued during the day
- The person you sleep with tells you your breathing changes as you sleep
- You have headaches or dry mouth when you wake in the morning
- Your memory is decreased, you are irritable or have frequent mood changes
- You wake frequently to urinate
- You snore

Although not everyone who experiences these has sleep apnea, these can be signs that sleep apnea is occurring.

If sleep apnea is found, the sleep specialist will recommend a CPAP (continuous positive airflow pressure) machine (or another, similar, option) that provides a constant stream of air into your throat, keeping your breathing passages open while you sleep.

Ultimately, however, the best way to deal with obstructive sleep apnea is to address the underlying cause. In many cases, the best way to do this is to lose weight.

Weight Gain

It's one thing to notice your clothes are fitting more tightly and you've gained a bit of weight. It's another thing to determine the cause so you can address it. While poor sleep plays a part in weight gain, it is more complex than that. There are number of possible factors that can influence your weight, and figuring out what they are is the best way to ensure successful weight loss.

How to Determine the Cause of Your Weight Gain

The standard theory for many years has been that 'calories in' (i.e. what you eat) should equal 'calories out' (i.e. the amount of energy you burn) in order to maintain your current weight.

Basically, the more you eat, the more energy you need to expend to avoid storage of those calories as body fat. This theory has some value, but it doesn't allow for the effect of hormones (such as cortisol, thyroid function and insulin), cellular metabolism, mitochondrial function, neurotransmitters, inflammatory messengers, leaky gut, and so on, which also influence your weight.

To fully understand weight gain, we need to look at what I refer to as your four core systems, which we'll discuss further in subsequent chapters:

1. Digestion

2. Immune system

3. Hormones

4. Nervous system

Then, we need to look at whether any of the three problem networks have developed, all of which can perpetuate imbalances in the four core systems:

1. Adrenal distress (discussed in Chapter 7)

2. Carbohydrate metabolism imbalances (discussed in Chapter 6)

3. Leaky gut (coming up in Chapter 10)

Once we know which of the networks is causing problems for you, we can make a weight loss plan tailored to you, rather than taking a cookie-cutter approach.

Balancing Hormones and Decreasing Inflammation

As we saw at the beginning of this chapter, the reason insomnia makes us gain weight is that it destabilizes the hormones that affect appetite, hunger and blood sugar, causing us to eat more and making it harder for our bodies to burn it off.

Knowing all this, let's look at how you can lose unwanted weight and prevent further weight gain with four steps that will help *rebalance* your hormones, while reducing the inflammation that results from the hormonal imbalance and contributes to weight gain.

Step 1: Make Your Blood Sugar Levels a Priority

First have your blood sugar levels tested (fasting blood sugar and hemoglobin A1c). Then if the levels are high, take steps to reduce your blood sugar levels. Drink water instead of sweetened beverages and alcohol, and eat something that contains protein and healthy fats at least every four hours (even on a busy day). Don't eat sugar or carbohydrates within three hours of going to sleep. By doing this, you'll reduce your blood sugar levels, while improving your insulin function. Remember to refer back to Chapter 6 for more tips.

Step 2: Identify Any Food Sensitivities and Heal Leaky Gut

Avoid any foods you are sensitive to in order to minimize inflammation and promote the healing of leaky gut. You can test for food sensitivities yourself, at home, with a simple finger-prick test. You can purchase a food sensitivities test from our website, or request one from your naturopathic doctor. We will discuss this further in Chapter 10.

Step 3: Know Your Cortisol Levels and Use Daily Stress Remedies

You can determine your cortisol levels by doing a saliva or urine panel, as explained in Chapter 7. Then, you can follow a course of action that lowers your cortisol and optimizes your stress response (this is fully explained in my book The Stress Remedy).

Step 4: Address Imbalanced Hormones and Neurotransmitters

Start by getting blood work done to evaluate thyroid function (TSH, free T4, free T3 and reverse T3), even slightly under functioning thyroid which is common with elevated cortisol, a urine test for estrogen, progesterone, testosterone, and melatonin, as well as a urine test for neurotransmitters. You'll learn more about these tests in subsequent chapters. Then you'll know exactly what kind of support your body needs.

Step 5: Sleep at an Incline

It is well established that sleeping at a 3 to 5 percent incline will assist with blood flow, lymph drainage and oxygenation of your body while you sleep. Check out the Samina bed in the resources section.

Creating a Plan for Weight Loss

As with any goal, it's important to break down your weight loss goals into "doable" steps. Choose goals that are achievable *for you*. It might be to lose two pounds by the end of the month. For others, it may be to lose ten pounds before an upcoming event. Note that these examples are also specific and should be tailored to your life. You can always adjust your goal if you find it is not achievable – that is part of the learning process.

Rather than simply reducing your calories (and risking sending your body into "starvation mode" and raising cortisol), I strongly recommend consulting with a naturopathic doctor before you embark on your weight loss journey. He/she can advise you on what, when and how much to eat to get the best results for your body.

Rather than embarking on a strict weight loss program, I recommend following a program, that guides you to address the three problem networks (adrenal distress, carbohydrate metabolism and leaky gut). By doing this you'll be losing weight because your body is getting healthier and your hormones are becoming more balanced.

The program I developed, called the Stress Remedy program, is a comprehensive approach to weight loss – including a meal plan, recipes and email tips – that support you to balance your blood sugar, avoid common food sensitivities including gluten, and to implement stress remedies that help you recover from adrenal distress.

Aim for Lasting Change

Whether you have sleep apnea or not, getting your body the support it needs to rebalance itself – whether that be adrenal support, leaky gut healing, blood sugar balancing, hormone or neurotransmitter balancing, or all of the above – will surely lead to improved sleep and health in general.

And while losing weight and overcoming sleep apnea might seem difficult at first, once you have achieved that balance, you will find it much easier to *stay* on track with your weight and your health, because you will finally be getting the precious sleep you need.

CHAPTER 9

How Inflammation and Pain Affect Your Sleep

In this chapter, we'll look at how inflammation and pain are common reasons for waking during the night, and explore some solutions to break the cycle.

What Do We Mean by Inflammation?

Let's start by understanding inflammation – what it is, where it's located, and how it can interfere with sleep.

We usually think of inflammation as redness, swelling and throbbing, such as when you stub your toe; but it can affect your internal organs, as well. Inflammation is an important part of the immune response that is involved in attracting the immune system to an area that needs to heal; it also protects an area that is damaged. It is your body's response to an injury, infection (even a common cold virus) or allergen.

Inflammation is, therefore, a good thing because it helps us recover and heal. However, it also has the potential to be detrimental to your health. *Chronic* inflammation (inflammation that sticks around for a long time and just won't go away) can lead to, and is involved in, many health issues and diseases, including heart disease, arthritis, asthma and diabetes.

Chronic inflammation can be caused by recurring physical or emotional stress, an imbalanced stress response and oxidative stress (stress at a cellular level).

The Problem with Inflammation

The problem is *cytokines*: "inflammatory messengers" that send signals anywhere in the body. These messengers can send signals to your heart, your cells and your nervous system. In fact, research is now showing that cytokines, and inflammation, are involved in anxiety and depression, as well as in obesity, heart disease, dementia and cancer.

So when you hear the word *inflammation*, don't just think of a painful, swollen joint; think of a *process* involving multiple factors that can either work for, or against, your health, and can go anywhere in your body, wherever you are most susceptible.

What Does This Have to Do with Your Sleep Problems?

Cytokines are also involved in insomnia. In a study[25] comparing normal sleepers to people with insomnia, it was found that normal cytokine levels were increased in those who were sleeping poorly, thus increasing inflammatory messages in the body.

It has also been found that chronic inflammation and elevated cytokines, from any cause, can lead to insomnia[26]. This means if you have inflammation as a result of arthritis, sinusitis, anxiety, or any other source of cytokines, you are more likely to have a hard time staying asleep – and to feel tired the next day.

Two other major, and often unrecognized, triggers of cytokines and inflammation that have the potential to influence sleep are food sensitivities and intestinal permeability, i.e. leaky gut. Food sensitivities are different from food allergies, although both cause inflammation. Food sensitivities cause inflammation in a more delayed, subtle way than allergies do, and are associated with over 200 different symptoms that can show up throughout the body for weeks after eating the food in question.

I'll be discussing food sensitivities in more depth in Chapter 10. In the meantime, I want to emphasize that when the intestinal lining is not as healthy as it could be, it allows food in your gut to trigger an immune response. When this happens, a cloud of inflammatory messengers (cytokines) can spread a signal of inflammation all the way to your nervous system, which can cause you to have a difficult time falling asleep, or can wake you up during the night.

So your sleep issue may be related to something you ate, or to the health of your digestion.

Then, of course, there is the pain associated with inflammation – whether from a sore back, stomach upset, or even head or nerve pain. This, too, can wake you with every move

75

you make. So, pain can make sleep difficult, and difficult sleep can increase pain – another vicious cycle that can be tough to break. It is only when we calm the inflammation, while also helping your body to heal, that you will be back to sleeping well.

How Can You Tell if You Have Inflammation?

Often we know simply based on the way you feel – your symptoms. However, there are blood tests for inflammation, including what is known as the SED rate, as well as C-reactive protein (CRP).

Because there are so many potential causes of inflammation, these tests can be vague, but they give a general sense of the degree of inflammation present. When inflammation is very high, these tests will clearly show it. Elevated levels of CRP are associated with heart disease, so this test is also used to assess heart disease risk. In the future, as research teaches us more about cytokine patterns, perhaps tests will be developed that allow us to relate cytokine levels to specific health issues, such as insomnia.

How Can We Resolve Inflammation?

Here are primary steps to resolving inflammation:

- **Identify sources of inflammation and address them.** If you have not yet been tested for food sensitivities, now is the time. This will tell you whether certain foods you are eating are maintaining the cycle of pain, inflammation and disrupted sleep. These tests will also give you a better sense of whether leaky gut is present, so you can start healing it. You can find out where to order a "finger-prick" food sensitivity kit in "Tests, Supplements and Where to Get Them" at the back of this book.

- **Avoid foods that are inflammatory.** The main foods to avoid or minimize are sugar, alcohol, dairy products (milk, cheese and yogurt), trans-fats (partially hydrogenated oils), processed foods, refined carbs (white bread, rice, potatoes and cereals), gluten (wheat, barley, rye and spelt), and red meat, as these are known to cause inflammation.

- **Choose foods that are anti-inflammatory.** Key anti-inflammatory foods are colorful fruits (berries, for example), vegetables (such as leafy greens), and healthy fats (like olive oil). The kinds of fats you eat is very important, as the body uses them to either increase or decrease inflammation. For example, the fats in fish (like salmon) and nuts (except for peanuts) are used to produce anti-inflammatory "messengers" in the body and protect your cells, whereas the fats in red meat (and other foods high in saturated fats) are used to make inflammatory cytokines. The same foods that decrease inflammation are often also high in anti-oxidants, which means they help block oxidative stress and decrease inflammation, as well.

- **Use anti-inflammatory herbs.** Many herbs are known to decrease inflammation, including turmeric (curcumin), boswellia, ginger and rosemary. These herbs can be taken individually or in combination, such as in products I frequently recommend called Zyflamend and InflaCalm.

- **Hemp oil containing cannabinoids** are also known to decrease inflammation. Find example products in the Resources section of this book.

- Use **anti-inflammatory enzymes.** When taken on an empty stomach, enzymes such as bromelain and pancreatic enzymes can also decrease inflammation in the body.

- **Drink water with electrolytes.** The way our body eliminates inflammation is through fluid. Having enough fluid and in balance with electrolytes will help your eliminate inflammation.

- **Address adrenal distress and cortisol imbalance.** Elevated cortisol levels will increase inflammation, so going back to address cortisol will help break the vicious cycle of inflammation. See chapter 7.

- **Sleep.** I know it may sound impossible, but my point is that be more we help you to get good sleep, the more we will decrease inflammation overall. That is because our bodies clear out inflammation even better while we sleep.

In some cases, say with a severe autoimmune flare or after a major injury, pain medications, anti-inflammatory medications (NSAIDS such as Ibuprofen and Aleve) or steroids (like prednisone) may be temporarily necessary to help calm down the inflammatory response and get you on the path to healing. My goal is to help you to be able to avoid inflammation and immune suppressive medications all together.

Diet and herbal approaches can be used in addition to and after the use of medications to support healing, ease the transition off medications and, ultimately, to improve sleep. Of course consult with your naturopathic doctor for any individual conflicts or potential contraindications.

As a naturopathic doctor my role is to help patients make changes to their diet and lifestyle, alongside using natural therapies to help speed their recovery. Whenever possible, I aim to decrease the need for medication, because long-term use of anti-inflammatory medications and/or steroids can damage the intestinal lining and lead to further inflammation.

Be Patient with the Healing Process

If you are caught in the vicious cycle of inflammation, pain and poor sleep, please know that it will take time to resolve. Cytokines and an immune system on high alert will only settle down as you address what triggered them in the first place. As time goes on, and with diligence, however, it is possible for your immune response to shift – even from autoimmunity – to healthy immune function.

Remember also that temporary changes in your normal routine, such as travel or the holidays, can increase inflammation and throw off your sleep. If this happens, you may want to consider taking a few days, a week or even three weeks to shift your diet away from inflammatory foods, and to support your body back to health.

CHAPTER 10

How Leaky Gut and Food Sensitivities Can Interfere with a Good Night's Sleep

At first, it might be hard to imagine what you eat could have anything to do with your sleep, but it does – in more ways than one.

So far, we've already discussed some of the food-related issues that can affect sleep:

- **Blood Sugar.** Sugar and high-carbohydrate foods cause your blood sugar levels to fluctuate, which can lead you to wake up during the night.

- **The hormone-weight-gain roller coaster.** *Leptin* and *ghrelin* are hormones related to appetite and hunger. When you don't sleep properly, the levels of these hormones shift, causing you to eat more. To make matters worse, insomnia makes your insulin less effective, so you end up gaining weight.

As we have discussed, weight gain can also disrupt sleep, thus creating a vicious cycle that is hard to break.

- **Inflammation.** Inflammation from any cause, including leaky gut and food sensitivities, can also affect our sleep. *Cytokines* (the "inflammatory messengers" that can tell any part of your body to become inflamed) are known to affect your ability to get a good night's sleep, and become imbalanced when you don't sleep well.

In this chapter, we'll take a more detailed look at how *cytokines* and inflammatory responses to foods (which start in the gut) have the potential to feed into the sleep-inflammatory pattern discussed in the previous chapter, further tilting the scale toward insomnia.

Of course, the less you sleep, the more likely you are to *crave* the foods that cause inflammation. So the better you understand what's going on, the more you will understand how to get off the food-inflammation-sleep loop.

Foods, Antibodies, Cytokines and Inflammation

When everything is working as it should, the food you eat is digested – first by your stomach acid, then by pancreatic enzymes, bile salts and the enzymes produced by the cells that line your intestines.

Food should not be allowed to travel through your intestinal wall unless it is digested down to the smallest molecules that can fit through the intestinal cells. However, when we are stressed and/or taking medications that block stomach acid production, the digestion of food isn't optimal and the cells lining the intestines are not as healthy. This is known as intestinal permeability or leaky gut.

Leaky gut can be mild, moderate or severe. In fact, considering the number of factors that cause leaky gut, it's clear that we all have some degree of leaky gut at any point in time. Your intestinal cells can also be compromised by gluten, pesticides, medications, alcohol, trauma and infections. And the more you consume foods you react to, the worse the leaky gut gets.

When partially undigested proteins are able to get through the leaky intestinal wall, the immune system identifies them as foreign substances that shouldn't be there and tries to protect you from them by making *cytokines* (inflammation signals) and antibodies (to attack) to the food.

Antibodies are part of our immune system. They show up when our immune system gets a signal that we are in danger of "attack" – when we catch a virus, for example. Ultimately, their role is to protect us from infections and disease.

Each antibody has a different job in our body. One antibody we hear about frequently is the IgE antibody, which can react when we have a severe allergy to certain foods (e.g. peanuts, shellfish, etc.) and can cause immediate, allergic type responses, such as hives and anaphylactic shock. IgE is the antibody allergists test for and address.

Two other antibodies – IgG and IgA – also respond to foods we eat. However, they don't trigger a severe allergic response; they trigger a delayed response over days to weeks. IgA antibodies tend to respond for up to a week after eating the problem food, whereas IgG can react for as long as three weeks after consumption. This delayed response can make it difficult for us to realize we have a sensitivity to a particular food.

As the antibodies respond to the food, inflammation increases, which may cause digestive symptoms, but not always. This means you may react to certain foods, but *never feel it* in your stomach. Instead, the inflammatory messages (cytokines) travel to other areas of your body, potentially resulting in headaches, joint pain, bladder discomfort and other health issues.

One of the most likely places these antibodies will create inflammation is your nervous system. This inflammation travels from your intestines, across the *blood-brain barrier,* and into your central nervous system. And when your nervous system is affected, it can lead to anxiety, depression, irritability, brain fog – and sleep issues.

Again, the purpose of cytokines is to protect the body from infection. But if cytokines start responding to foods you eat every day, they can disrupt the careful balance of your nervous system. This is referred to as the gut-brain axis, which is how inflammation from your gut causes issues in your nervous system. Cortisol and a stress response is also triggered, further perpetuating the effect of stress.

If food sensitivities and leaky gut (plus imbalanced gut bacteria we'll discuss soon) go unaddressed, it can in some cases also lead to an auto-immune response – when your body starts attacking its own tissue, instead of just the offending foods. In fact more and more research points to leaky gut as the underlying cause of autoimmune conditions such as Hashimoto's thyroiditis, rheumatoid arthritis, lupus, multiple sclerosis, Behcet's and more, many of which have insomnia as a confounding health issue.

The Most Common Offenders

Gluten and dairy proteins (not lactose, but casein and whey) are two of the most common food sensitivities.

In particular, gluten (and wheat in general) cannot be completely digested by humans, so if you eat it often, and especially if you have a genetic tendency to react to gluten, your immune system is likely to kick in and start having inflammatory responses to gluten.

Research has shown that gluten – in barley, rye, spelt and wheat – is known to cause leaky gut **whether or not you have celiac disease or gluten sensitivity**[27, 28].

It does this by increasing a protein called *zonulin* that opens up spaces between the cells lining the intestines, making it easier for food molecules to leak into the blood stream.

Gluten, therefore, can be responsible for generating an ever-increasing number of food sensitivities (also referred to as cross-reactions). If this reason alone were not enough to encourage us to avoid it, studies have shown that gluten is also known to increase inflammation in the nervous system[29].

It is also worth noting that sleep issues are very common for people who have gluten sensitivity or celiac disease.

Dairy products – i.e. products made from cow's milk – can be an issue for many people for several reasons. One we hear about most often is an inability to digest lactose, which is the "sugar" in dairy products. When lactose is not digested well, it can cause digestive upset including bloating, cramping and bowel changes.

The proteins in dairy (casein and whey) can also be an issue if they are not digested well; if the undigested proteins leak though the intestinal lining, it can trigger an immune response. When antibodies from the immune system respond to dairy proteins, it can cause digestive upset and/or inflammatory symptoms anywhere in your body, from joint pain and sinus congestion, to mood and sleep changes.

Breaking the Cycle Once and for All

Ridding your body of inflammation requires some detective work to determine the causes, followed by a systematic method for healing leaky gut. Below is my step-by-step approach.

Step 1: Do an IgG and IgA Food Sensitivity Panel

You could try to guess which foods to avoid (gluten and dairy products are the most likely culprits), but it's so easy to get tested and find out for sure. Plus, when we find IgG and IgA antibodies to foods, it also gives an indication of leaky gut. Think of it this way - our immune system only reacts to foods when the intestinal cells allow food to leak through to the immune system. So if you react, it means the intestinal lining is leaky.

There are many food sensitivity panels out there, but I find the clearest place to start is with an IgG and IgA panel. IgG and IgA antibodies may or may not react to the same foods, so I always recommend testing them both.

IgG and IgA panels aren't usually offered by standard labs; if they are, they frequently only test for a few foods. So the best way to get a thorough panel done is to see a naturopathic or functional medicine practitioner.

I recommend an IgG and IgA panel done with a finger-prick blood sample from a lab I've found to be highly accurate. You can do this test in the comfort of your own home and send it to the laboratory through the mail. The lab will check your sample against 96 of the most common foods, including gluten and dairy, to find out if your immune system is attacking the food you are eating.

You can read more about this test (and find out how to order it) in "Tests, Supplements and Where to Get Them" at the back of this book.

Step 2: Eliminate the Reactive Foods

Some of the test results will be straightforward: do you react or not? If you react, then the best way to decrease inflammation in your body is to avoid that food – it's that simple. Take away what is triggering an immune response, and you've eliminated the response and allowed for greater recovery.

However, some patterns in the results may not be self-evident. Gluten sensitivity, for example, can exist even with a *low* reactivity to gluten. That's why you might find it useful to talk through the results with a specialist who can help you interpret your results and advise you on dietary changes.

Be sure to refer to my suggestions later in this chapter and in the resources section of the book in order to help you to be successful.

Step 3: Digest at Your Best

Ensuring you take time to chew your food thoroughly and not eat too much food (especially carbohydrates) at one sitting will give your body a better chance of digesting well.

Additionally, we can support each aspect of your digestion using plant-based enzymes, hydrochloric acid, and/or bile support depending on your needs. To be thorough, it is best to meet with a naturopathic doctor and complete a specialized stool test in order to find out how well you are digesting proteins, carbohydrates and fats to know what support is needed for your body.

As a first step, I recommend taking plant-based pancreatic enzymes with meals to support the digestion of food. Pancreatic enzymes can help digest proteins, fats and carbohydrates, ensuring that you can absorb the nutrients and avoid immune responses to the foods you eat.

An example product that I recommend is called Enzyme Support. Enzyme Support is designed to digest all food types and it also contains the specific enzymes to digest gluten and casein (the protein in dairy products) in case you are exposed to them. It won't be able to digest a whole piece of bread, but can help prevent issues from small exposures.

Step 4: Ingest the Solution

Addressing and healing leaky gut is really the only way to stop your ongoing food sensitivity issues. Your immune system should really **not** be reacting to the foods you eat; it shouldn't even be coming into contact with them. So to truly resolve this problem, you need to *heal your intestinal lining* to prevent other food reactions in the future.

While you are giving your body a rest from reactive foods, you can speed the healing of leaky gut by taking nutrients and herbs.

First I focus on the amino acid that is such an important fuel to the small intestinal cells, L-glutamine. By taking glutamine (up to about 3000 mg per day) you'll be feeding the cells that line your intestines and helping them to recover from leaky gut.

Next we add in anti-inflammatory herbs that support a natural healing process such as licorice (DGL), quercetin, aloe, slippery elm, and/or curcumin. We could also add MSM (methylsulfonylmethane), which provides sulfur that helps the tight junctions between the cells to heal and zinc which is essential for healthy new cells in the intestinal lining. By taking these supplements orally, we can get all of them to the location of leaky gut—the small intestines.

When leaky gut is more severe (and your digestion is more sensitive), it can be necessary to start simple with one ingredient at a time. For others a combination formula can make it possible to take in several supportive herbs and nutrients in one product.

Find some of the specific formulas I recommend here:

- Glutamine alone: L-GLUTAMINE POWDER and capsules
- DGL alone: DGL POWDER

- Glutamine in combination with aloe and DGL as a powder: DR. DONI'S LEAKY GUT SUPPORT
- Glutamine in combination with herbs and nutrients as a capsule: GI REPAIR NUTRIENTS

Step 5: Optimize Healthy Bacteria

There are several possible scenarios in which the bacteria (referred to as microbiome or microbiota) that should be healthfully living in your large intestines can be thrown off track (known as dysbiosis).

You could have taken a lot of antibiotics that killed the healthy bacteria and allowed yeast (also known as candida) to grow in its place. Or perhaps you've overdone the fermented foods such as sauerkraut, kombucha, and yogurt and they've become too happy in a place that requires a careful balance of the right bacteria.

If you are experiencing gas, bloating, burping, discomfort, constipation, loose stools, or any other digestive distress, it is quite likely that the bacteria living in your intestines are not in an optimal balance. Overgrowing bacteria produce toxins that further exacerbate leaky gut and inflammation throughout your body and nervous system - referred to as the "microbiota-gut-brain connection" - so it is imperative to address them.

The way to find out is do tests that tell us about your gut bacteria. To understand the bacteria in the small intestines, we do a breath test that measures the amount of gases produced by bacteria. If the gas (hydrogen and/or methane) is elevated, we know there is an overgrowth of bacteria to address (called SIBO or small intestinal bacterial overgrowth).

To know about the bacteria in the large intestine, a stool panel is needed, but not just any stool test. You'll want to do a specialty stool panel that is able to identify the bacteria based on their DNA. Remember, there are trillions of bacteria living in our intestines and they don't all grow in a culture. By doing a genetically-based test (referred to as PCR) we can get a much better sense of whether there are over or under growing bacteria and therefore what is needed in order to bring them back to balance.

Once we know more about any imbalance of bacteria in your gut, we can start to change the environment so the healthiest bacteria are able to flourish and protect your body. I guide patients through a process of addressing overgrowing bacteria (or yeast) using herbs, nutrients, as well as specific types of bacteria that help address imbalances. I call them "traffic directors" because they help guide the overgrowing bacteria to leave and the good bacteria to stay.

To get started with a high-quality probiotic (if you'd like to try something before going down the path of finding a practitioner and doing a stool test), I recommend PROBIOTIC SUPPORT. It contains 2 strains of Lactobacillus and 1 strain of Bifidobacteria that are known to decrease inflammation and improve the balance of bacteria in the intestines.

If you ever feel worse after taking a probiotic or prebiotic, you should stop taking it and consult with a naturopathic doctor who can help you assess the cause and best approach for you. In many cases it is multi-step process. While it can seem daunting at first, I assure you it is possible to rebalance the gut bacteria.

Keep in mind, however, that healthy bacteria require a healthy intestinal lining, so addressing leaky gut and stabilizing your digestion is an ongoing process alongside maintaining the right balance of gut bacteria.

Bacteria also need to be fed so that they can produce the nutrients and short chain fatty acids that are beneficial to our colon and body in general. "Pre-biotics" the term used to describe food for our bacteria and includes fiber of various types, such as fiber from fruits, vegetables, nuts and seeds. Essentially the bacteria living in our intestines are determined by the foods we eat. When we eat healthy, high-fiber foods, we grow healthy bacteria to help keep us healthy and sleeping well.

How Long to Avoid the Foods and Heal Leaky Gut?

If you have already done a food sensitivities test and discovered which foods are triggering your immune system, your next goal should be to avoid those foods while you are working towards healing any leaky gut issues that may be contributing to your sleeplessness. To be thorough, it's always best to avoid those foods for **six months to a year** before re-testing.

If you haven't taken a food sensitivities test (or you don't want to), you could try eliminating the "usual suspects": gluten and dairy. If that's the path you choose, be sure to avoid these foods for a minimum of three weeks. However, many people with severe food sensitivities will need to eliminate these foods for at least **three months** before they note a significant difference. Remember, these sensitivities may have been troubling you for many years, so you need to give your body time to heal.

Once you feel better (or when your naturopathic doctor advises you to do so), you can carry out a "reintroduction challenge" to see how your body responds. This entails eating ONE serving of a food type you've been avoiding. Then, over the next few days, you wait and observe to see if there are any changes in the way you feel or in how well you are sleeping. You will soon learn whether or not you are able to tolerate this food in your diet.

After you have determined how well (or not) you are responding to one of the previously eliminated foods, follow the same process with the next food type. If you find you do react or feel worse in any way, you know you are still sensitive to that food and you should continue to avoid it. As your leaky gut heals, you'll become less reactive to the offending foods, and more likely to be able to add them back without experiencing any negative symptoms (with the exception of gluten which causes leaky gut and remains a risk or stress factor to avoid).

What Do Foods Have to Do With Sleep?

It may be hard to believe that foods have anything to do with sleep, but they most definitely do.

As we've discussed in this chapter, you might be eating foods that are leaking through your intestinal lining, causing inflammation and disturbing your sleep.

That said, I encourage you not to try to make these changes on your own, but to work with a naturopathic doctor or holistic nutritionist who can ensure the diet changes you make still allow you to get important nutrients.

One option is to follow the Stress Remedy 21-day program that I designed. It includes a gluten-free, dairy-free meal plan and recipes. Plus it comes with daily email tips and access to a private Facebook group. You could then use an organic pea protein shake, enzymes with meals, leaky gut healing powder, and probiotics to further support healing your gut.

Healing food sensitivities is NOT a "quick fix." It takes time to make changes to what you eat, and it takes time for your body to bring itself back into balance. But have faith! Addressing your food sensitivities can not only lead to better sleep, but can also put your overall health on a much better path.

For more comprehensive support, I also offer a complete Leaky Gut and Digestive Solutions Package, which includes the food sensitivity panel and several consultations with me to support you with the process of healing leaky gut.

You can read about the mentioned products and services in the appendices at the back of this book.

CHAPTER 11

How Imbalanced Neurotransmitters Affect Your Sleep

In this chapter, we will look at how inflammation affects the *nervous* system, how the delicate balance of the biochemical messengers in our nervous system (neurotransmitters) can be thrown off track and how taking the right nutrients can help bring them back into balance.

What Are Neurotransmitters?

Neurotransmitters are like hormones, except they work specifically within the nervous system. The nervous system affects mood, energy levels, sleep and mental focus. The great thing about neurotransmitters is that they are all made in our body with nutrients. This means *we can shift them through the use of nutrients.*

When I discuss wakeful sleep with patients, although they have a sense that the cause of their sleep problems might have something to do with a racing mind, they usually don't consider that it might have anything to do with their nervous system or that there are options besides medications.

Perhaps because the nervous system is thought of as a far-off, untouchable location in the body, many people believe they have no control over neurotransmitters such as serotonin, dopamine, GABA and glutamate – but we *do*.

Measuring Neurotransmitters in Your Body

It is possible to measure the levels of neurotransmitters in your system from a simple urine sample, and to address imbalances using the right nutrients and herbs30. (Examples of these products can be found at the end of this book.)

Sadly, only a few specialty labs offer this service, and most practitioners are unaware of the availability and usefulness of the test, even though it has been available for clinical use for over a decade.

I've been intrigued by neurotransmitters and urine testing for over fifteen years. In lectures to health professionals and in an article I published in 2009, I have presented what I've found, through my practice, to be one of the keys to success with many health issues, including anxiety, depression (and post-partum depression), PMS/PMDD and insomnia – the careful balancing of neurotransmitters (and cortisol) with the use of nutrients and herbs.

First, what is evident in the research is that many neurological and mental health conditions, including insomnia, are caused by inflammation in the nervous system[31]. This inflammation often originates in the gut and spreads through the blood/brain barrier to the nervous system (as discussed in a prior chapter).

In this situation, it is likely that something you are eating is causing the inflammation and is directly responsible for throwing off your sleep and your mood. Stress itself, whether physical or emotional, can also increase inflammation and disrupt neurotransmitter levels.

While it can sound pretty awful, the good thing is that we can ***do something about it***. Once we know what's causing the problem, we can make changes to rectify the situation. We can change what we eat and we can take additional nutrients to help rebalance our neurotransmitter levels and bring them back to normal.

What Do Neurotransmitters Actually Do?

Put very simply, neurotransmitters either stimulate or calm us, and it's important to have a balance between the two. If you have too much of the stimulating neurotransmitters during the day, it could cause anxiety; at night, it could wake you from your sleep with thoughts of what you need to get done, or even give you nightmares. On the other hand, if you have too little of the calming neurotransmitters, you may feel jittery and restless.

It's not possible to guess whether you have too much stimulation or too little calm. The only way to know for sure is to measure your levels. In many cases, I find there is more than one imbalance of the neurotransmitters in the nervous system. For example:

- **Serotonin** is a calming neurotransmitter and if you have too little, it can cause sleep issues (this is common if you have leaky gut, as 90% of serotonin is made in the gut).

- If, at the same time, your **glutamate** (the most stimulatory neurotransmitter) levels are too high, your mind will be racing right when it's time to sleep.

- Combine this with a high **cortisol** level at night (when it should be low) and you're sure to be up all night.

Balancing your neurotransmitters is a complex and delicate process that often requires fine-tuning and adjusting to match your body's needs. It's too much to try to sort out on your own – it's far better to work with a practitioner who is trained in the use of nutrients and herbs that support you back to balance.

Start by Calming Your Nervous System

When working with neurotransmitters, it's always important to start by *calming* the nervous system first. Whether you need to increase your GABA (a very calming neurotransmitter that I refer to as your "stress buffer") or lower your **adrenaline** (a stimulating neurotransmitter:

think stress, fight or flight), we'll always begin by calming your nervous system before moving onto the next step.

A perfect example is (again) **serotonin**. It is made in the body from the amino acid **tryptophan**, which is turned into **5-HTP** (5-hydroxytryptophan), which is, in turn, made into serotonin. For some people, especially when serotonin levels are extremely low, it is important to start by taking tryptophan, even though more steps are required to convert it into serotonin, because a more gradual transition is needed. Others can start right in by taking 5-HTP, which is why you'll often find it in sleep formulas and protocols.

I suggest first testing your levels, and then working with a practitioner who can help you tso figure out whether you need serotonin support, and how to support it in the best way for you. NOTE: It is particularly important to check with your prescribing doctor before taking 5HTP if you are taking a psychotropic medication such as an SSRI or SNRI because it is possible to support serotonin too much.

Magnesium is often depleted when we are exposed to high amounts of stress. Taking magnesium supplements, especially in the form of magnesium glycinate or threonate (versus citrate and oxide) can help calm your nervous system by aiding in processing adrenaline and relaxing your muscles. I often recommend a product called Magnesium Plus, which contains both magnesium and vitamin B6.

Vitamin B6 (also known as P5P in the active form) can also be calming because it helps your body to process (and reduce excess amounts of) adrenaline and to support sero-tonin levels. Again, I recommend the product Magnesium Plus, which contains both magnesium and vitamin B6.

Theanine supports levels of GABA, a calming neu-rotransmitter in the body, helping with mood, focus, memo-ry, and relaxation.

GABA is a neurotransmitter that can be taken as a sup-plement. When you are healthy, it is not well absorbed into the nervous system, but when the blood-brain barrier is leaky (due to inflammation and stress), then GABA is thought to be transported to the brain where it can help calm anxiety. Another way it can calm the nervous system is by interacting with bacteria in your digestive tract. It's best to try it and see how well it works for you. There are also supplements that combine GABA with theanine for greater effectiveness.

Hemp oil and cannabinoids have been shown to help calm the nervous system, which can help with sleep and anx-iety. Many hemp oil and cannabinoid products are available in liquid, capsule and topical forms. I recommend starting with a low dose, during the day so you can see how your body responds, and then you can modify the dose and shift it to bedtime for optimal results. Refer to the Resources section of the book for details.

Herbs that are calming to the nervous system:

Chamomile (such as a tea)

Lavender (essential oil or capsule form)

Hops (or "humulus"), an ingredient in beer, is calming to the nervous system. It is often used in combination products (see below).

Passion flower (or "passiflora") has a gentle calming effect on the nervous system.

Valerian root

California poppy

Lemon Balm

Step 2: Improve Adrenal Gland Function and Methylation

Once you are calmer, and hopefully sleeping through the night, it's time to move on to the next step in helping your body recover: restoring optimal adrenal function and methylation.

Be sure to go back to Chapter 7 where we discussed recovery from adrenal distress.

Next is something called "methylation," which is what B vitamins do in our bodies. The B vitamins join together in a process called methylation that results in the production of something called methionine. Methionine and SAM (s-adenosyl methionine) are used throughout the body to make healthy cells, neurotransmitters and to metabolize neurotransmitters and toxins. Without enough B vitamins (in the active form) or if you have genetic variations (SNPs) that influence methylation, that could result in imbalanced neurotransmitter levels.

Again, it is important to work with a practitioner who has been trained in the most effective ways to address both adrenal distress and methylation issues. You may want to complete a genetic panel to access your genetic data so that you know whether you are predisposed to methylation issues.

Be Sure to Work with an Experienced Practitioner

As you can see, addressing neurotransmitter issues is very complex, and I don't recommend trying to do all this on your own. Be sure to work with an experienced naturopathic doctor or other practitioner who can take all your individual circumstances into account – including any medications you may be taking that might have an effect or interact with the herbs and nutrients.

Taking It S-L-O-W

Getting your neurotransmitters back in balance can take anywhere from four weeks to four years. It really depends on your body – its health issues and how it responds to change. As tempting as it may be to quickly raise the neurotransmitters that were low, this could be a shock to your system and can create even more problems. So be patient, and make sure to pace yourself and take it slow.

Once your neurotransmitters do come back into balance, you'll not only sleep a lot better at night, but you'll be sending a balanced message throughout your body, improving your digestion, immune function, hormone levels, mood and much more.

CHAPTER 12

HORMONES AND SLEEP DISRUPTION – PREGNANCY, POSTPARTUM, PERI-MENOPAUSE AND MENOPAUSE

In this chapter, we'll be looking at how changes in estrogen and progesterone levels can affect sleep for women, and what you can do about it.

Estrogen, Progesterone and Sleep

The hormones that orchestrate the benefits of sleep can be disrupted by other hormone changes in the body, such as when estrogen and progesterone levels fluctuate or shift. This is why insomnia is so common among women who are pregnant, postpartum, during peri-menopause (leading up to menopause) and after.

Estrogen and **progesterone** are the hormones produced by the ovaries, creating a menstrual cycle in women aged (on average) between ages 12 and 51. Estrogen signals to the

107

uterus to grow blood vessels in preparation for a possible pregnancy. Progesterone, which is produced after ovulation (when the ovaries release an egg) each month, maintains the uterine lining for the next two weeks in case a pregnancy occurs.

If pregnancy does not happen, progesterone levels drop, allowing the uterine lining to slough, what we refer to as a menses or "period." This cycle optimally lasts 28 days, between the first day of the period and the first day of the next period.

But that's not the only effect of estrogen and progesterone in a woman's body. These hormones actually influence many other areas of the body including the nervous system, immune system, digestion, and other hormones (thyroid, insulin, and cortisol, for example).

Optimally, estrogen and progesterone should be in balance with one another; when they are out of balance or simply changing – as they do in pregnancy, postpartum, during the menstrual cycle, and as the ovaries decrease in function with age – women can feel the effects throughout their bodies.

Common symptoms of hormonal changes:

- **Mood** – Irritability, low mood, anxiety, and libido changes

- **Digestion** – Change in bowel movements and ability to digest, bloating

- **Skin** – Acne and other skin issues

- **Joints** – Aches and pains

- **Blood Vessels** – Hot flashes, night sweats, and migraines

- **Metabolism** – Decreased insulin function and increased weight gain (especially around your middle)

- **Breasts** – Tenderness, cysts, pain

- **Vaginal** – Dryness, susceptibility to infection, discharge changes

- **Urinary** – Frequent urination, discomfort, susceptibility to infection

And finally…

- **Sleep** – Inability to get to sleep, frequent waking, can't get back to sleep

Estrogen, the Full Story

We often talk about estrogen as a single hormone, but there are actually three forms:

1. **Estrone** (the strongest form)

2. **Estradiol** (the most prevalent form in menstruating women)

3. **Estriol** (the weakest of the three, and more prevalent in menopause)

All forms of estrogen are metabolized by the liver and leave the body in bile that travels from the gall bladder out through the bowels. Each of us has a unique ability to metabolize (or detoxify) estrogen in the liver in two phases, including a process called **methylation**.

The efficiency with which we do this is determined by our genetics. If your body is not as able to detoxify estrogen well, it will stay in your body longer and in more toxic forms, increasing the risk of PMS and fibroids, as well as breast cancer and other estrogen-related health issues like endometriosis.

Once estrogens get to the intestines, it important that they are bound by fiber in order to be removed from the digestive tract via the stool. This is referred to as phase 3 of detoxification. Otherwise estrogens can be reabsorbed into the body and recirculate through, perpetuating an imbalance in hormone levels and making more work for your liver.

When estrogen is higher than progesterone for any reason, including peri-menopause, the menstrual cycle becomes irregular – either shorter or longer than 28 days. Symptoms of premenstrual syndrome (PMS) – such as mood changes, bloating, breast tenderness and water retention – become more likely. Menstrual cramping, fibroids, polyps and heavy bleeding are also more likely when estrogen is higher than progesterone (known as estrogen dominance).

What happens with Sleep During and After Pregnancy

During pregnancy, both estrogen and progesterone increase, which can also disrupt sleep. I remember waking in the middle of the night, while pregnant, as awake as if it was day time. I tried to go back to sleep, but the issue is that there are few things that are okay to take while pregnant. So instead, I allowed "nesting" to happen in preparation for my daughter's birth. Nesting is a natural process by which our bodies get us ready for a baby to arrive.

Then once baby is born, the levels drop, creating yet another shift in sleep patterns. There can be sweating (which means you'll be able to see your ankles again!) and waking to breastfeed. Sleep support and training for baby can make a difference (see resources section). Otherwise you may experience what I refer to as "imposed insomnia" - when another person (a baby) disrupts your sleep leading to the same symptoms that occur with insomnia (fatigue and brain fog, to name a couple).

In my case, we tried most everything and my daughter would only sleep when next to me, so that is what we did. Co-sleeping is considered to be safe and supportive for children as they grow and mature. I chose to use the time in bed with my daughter to write my first book - The Stress Remedy.

What Happens with Peri-menopause

Symptoms of peri-menopause can begin as much as ten years before the menstruation ceases altogether (menopause is marked by one year without a period). Most commonly, progesterone levels begin to decrease first, especially when women are stressed, because both age and stress decrease the amount of progesterone produced by the ovaries. This creates an imbalance between progesterone and estrogen.

Eventually, as peri-menopause progresses, the ovaries also start to make less estrogen, so both progesterone and estrogen levels gradually decrease. Estrogen often decreases in a turbulent manner, sometimes fluctuating from high to low within minutes. Every time estrogen levels shift, it sends a signal through your body that triggers many of the symptoms we associate with peri-menopause or menopause – insomnia, night sweats, hot flashes, migraines, and mood changes.

When ovulation finally stops altogether, estrogen and progesterone levels stop cycling from low to high, and remain low. At this point women are likely to experience vaginal dryness, urinary infections, joint pain, and weight gain – all of which can disrupt sleep.

Is There a Test that Can Tell Me What's Going On?

Estrogen and progesterone levels can be measured in the blood, urine and saliva. Each test is used for different purposes and, of course, the timing of the test (based on ovulation) directly influences the levels:

- **Blood tests** show the level of estrogen (or, more specifically, of estrone, estradiol and estriol) and progesterone at the time the blood is drawn and can help identify levels that are very high or too low.

- **Salivary tests** can be helpful, especially when levels are measured in a series, over several days or a whole month, to identify patterns.

- **Urine samples** can be collected over 24 hours, but my preference is as dried urine on strips (referred to as a DUTCH test), to show estrogen and progesterone levels, and also how well they are being metabolized or detoxified by the liver.

A practitioner with training in the use of these tests will be able to tell you if testing is right for you and, if so, which test will be most helpful. You can read about some of the tests we offer through our own practice in "Tests, Supplements and Where to Get Them" at the back of this book.

A **genetic panel,** such as the one I discussed in an article about MTHFR mutations, can tell you whether you have genetic mutations that can affect your ability to detoxify estrogen and process it out of your body. If you do have these mutations, we can support your body with nutrients, herbs and other supplements, to decrease your risk of developing health issues such as PMS, fibroids, endometriosis, and even insomnia.

It can also be helpful to measure **cortisol** and **neurotransmitter** levels when addressing estrogen and progesterone. Neurotransmitters and hormones affect each other, which means that balancing one will automatically benefit the other. Again, you can find out where to get those kinds of tests at the back of this book.

What Can I Do if Hormonal Changes Affect My Sleep?

When it comes to helping you get back to sleep even while your hormones are changing (whether as a result of your menstrual cycle, after pregnancy, peri-menopause or post-menopause), there are many nutrients, herbs and supplements that can help. I've separated them into three categories:

1. Estrogen Support
2. Progesterone Support
3. Detoxification of Estrogen Support

Below is a list of recommended supplements for each of these categories, with a brief explanation of what each one does.

Estrogen Support (When Levels Are Too Low, such as peri-menopause)

- Black Cohosh (**Cimicifuga**) – This is one of the most studied and clinically effective herbs to assist with hot flashes, night sweats and other peri—menopausal symptoms. Black cohosh used to be considered a "phyto-estrogen" (a naturally occurring nutrient that mimics the effects of estrogen) but is now believed to be more of an estrogen blocker, by taking up space in the estrogen receptors. It has been shown to be safe for patients who have, or who have had, breast cancer.

- Maca – Becoming increasingly popular lately, Maca has been well researched and is considered safe and effective for PMS, perimenopausal and post-menopausal symptoms. It helps to balance hormones and, in particular, supports estrogen levels that are too low.

Progesterone Support

- Chaste Tree Berry **(Vitex)** – One of my "go to" herbs whenever we need to support the ovaries to ovulate and produce hormones on their own, Chaste Tree Berry assists with the communication from the brain to the ovaries, resulting in increased progesterone production.

- **Wild Yam (Dioscorea)** – Wild yam, both in oral and topical forms, acts as a mild progesterone-like substance in the body. Wild yam (and several other plants) make hormone-like substances, which can then be turned into "natural" or "bio-identical" progesterone that looks and acts the same as the progesterone our bodies make.

- **Progesterone Cream** – Derived from plant sources, and then modified in a lab to form "natural" or "bio-identical" progesterone (meaning it looks and behaves the same as the progesterone our bodies make), progesterone cream can be applied topically as a way to support low progesterone levels.

- **Adrenal Support, which Supports Healthy Ovarian Function** – When the adrenal glands are under-functioning, the ovaries may also produce too little estrogen and progesterone. In those cases, assessing and addressing adrenal function can greatly improve peri-menopausal and post-menopausal symptoms.

Detoxification of Estrogens (NOT while breastfeeding)

- **B Vitamins:** B6 (P5P), folate (5MTHF), and B12 – B vitamins, and especially B6, B12 and folate, are needed by the liver to detoxify estrogens.

- **Methylation Support: Choline, SAMe** – Methylation is an important step in the detoxification of estrogens. Choline and SAMe provide methyl groups for that process.

- Diindolmethionine (DIM) and Sulfurophane – Substances that come from broccoli, including indole-3 carbinol, diindolmethionine and sulfurophane, are all known to assist in the detoxification of estrogens, ensuring they exit the body instead of being converted into toxic estrogens that can cause health issues.

- **Calcium D-Glucarate** - assists with removing estrogens from the body through the stool, otherwise estrogens can be reabsorbed and recirculated through the body, adding to the total estrogen load.

- **Turmeric (Curcumin)** – Shown in research to support the detoxification of many substances, including estrogen.

- **Milk Thistle (Silymarin)** – Milk Thistle is generally supportive of liver detoxification and is known to assist with ridding the body of excess estrogens.

- Green Tea Extract – Studies show that green tea extract (also known as EGCG) can help detoxify toxins and estrogens from the body, and decrease the negative effects of excess estrogen.

- Fiber, such as ground flaxseeds - To help bind estrogens in the digestive tract and ensure that they are eliminated.

There are also combination products that contain ingredients from each of these categories. You can find links to purchase these products in "Test, Supplements and Where to Get Them" at the back of this book.

Men

Men can also experience hormone changes and sleep issues as a result. As men age, they too have a reduction in hormone production that can influence sleep. If you think this may be the case, I encourage you to seek out the help of a naturopathic doctor who can test your hormone levels and get you the support you need.

Guiding You to Hormone Balance

If you have a feeling hormone changes may be affecting your sleep, try taking herbs that help balance the hormones. If you find this isn't enough to get you back to sleeping well, it can be helpful to do a dried urine test to measure your estrogen, progesterone and testosterone levels, as well as how your body is metabolizing the hormones, in order to identify exactly where the issue is occurring. Once you have this information, you'll be able to choose a product that addresses the issue more specifically.

However, balancing estrogen and progesterone can be a challenge, and it is often much easier if you have a practitioner helping you wade through all those complexities. As with everything else we've discussed throughout this book, the length of time to correct an imbalance depends entirely on your body, and whether there are other underlying issues such as cortisol, leaky gut and nutrient depletions. Some patients see significant changes within a single month, while others will have a longer journey back to hormonal stability.

Once again, have patience – and have faith. While your hormone imbalances might make you *feel* like you're losing your grip on life, your naturopathic doctor can guide you gently, naturally and scientifically back to where you feel like yourself again – and sleep more soundly at night.

CHAPTER 13

How Low Melatonin Can Affect Your Sleep

In this chapter, we will look at **melatonin**: the hormone we rely on to create our circadian rhythm (sleep-wake cycle) and give us the benefits of sleep.

It's amazing how our bodies respond to light and darkness! As the day comes to an end, our eyes pick up the change from light to darkness and send a signal to the pineal gland in the brain to start producing a hormone called melatonin.

Each hormone communicates different messages within our bodies; melatonin's main message is sleep. As melatonin levels increase and start circulating through our bodies, we become sleepy. As you might guess, melatonin levels are highest in the evening (around 10 pm) and lowest during the day.

In addition to telling our bodies when it's time to sleep, melatonin is also an anti-oxidant – quenching the oxidative stress that damages our cells – and it influences our immune system and mood. It's a clever hormone with a raft of possible benefits, including:

- Helping with depression and seasonal affective disorder (SAD)[32, 33]

- Helping relieve pain (such as with fibromyalgia)[34]

- Preventing a build up of amyloid plaque associated with Alzheimer's disease[35]

- Preventing and even eliminating cancer cells[36]

- Decreasing the influence estrogen has on tumor growth[37]

This last point is why melatonin is so often recommended by practitioners who are supporting patients who have, or have had, cancer – especially breast cancer.

Understanding the benefits of melatonin helps us see why lack of sleep is so damaging. The biggest concern is when melatonin levels are too low in the evening, when they should be high enough to send you to sleep for the night. When this happens, you are left vulnerable to both the effects of lack of sleep and the effects of a lack of melatonin.

The good news is that it doesn't have to stay that way – you can correct your melatonin levels by addressing the *cause* of low levels.

What Causes Melatonin to Be Low (When It Should Be High)?

There are a number of things that influence melatonin production, including:

- Stress

- Lack of exposure to natural light during the day[38]

- Exposure to light at night (often from television, phones, computers and clocks)[39,]

- Working a night shift

- Travel and time zone changes (also known as jet lag)

- Lack of sleep (e.g. parents who are up every night with an infant/child)

- Leaky gut and nutrient deficiencies (nutrients are needed to make melatonin)

- Amyloid plaque

- Genetic tendencies

Studies have found that there are genes that influence our circadian rhythm, which means that you could have a predisposition to a shifted sleep-wake cycle, making you more likely to experience insomnia. We can find this out by doing a genetic panel and then running it through a software program that tells us about your genes.

Now remember that our genes are not the only influence on our health, in fact they are likely less than 25% of the determining factors. So if you have genes that could affect your circadian rhythm, don't give up. You can still influence your sleep with the tips I have for you below.

How Will I Feel if My Melatonin Is Low (When It Should Be High)?

There are a number of possible symptoms and everyone is different, but if you experience more than one of the following, your melatonin levels may be out and it might be worth considering getting tested:

- Feeling awake instead of sleepy after 10 pm
- Finding it hard to get to sleep
- Feeling tired during the day
- Forgetfulness
- Higher susceptibility to colds and flu (lower immunity)

How Can I Find Out if My Melatonin Levels Are Too Low?

As you've already learned, I'm a big fan of testing. The test for melatonin levels is simple: you collect a saliva or urine sample at about 10 pm to see what your melatonin level is when it should be at its highest. It can also be helpful to see what your melatonin level is right before you go to sleep (if that is different from 10 pm).

Unfortunately, this test is not commonly offered in a standard medical office or in sleep clinics, so you'll need to work with a naturopathic doctor, or functional medicine practitioner, who can do the test, interpret the results and advise you on the support you need to get your melatonin levels back in balance.

Support and Treatment for Low Melatonin

Here are four simple things you can do if you have low melatonin, to help you get a good night's sleep:

1. **Turn out the lights before 10 pm.** Some sources even recommend turning down the lights at sunset or by 7 pm. I recommend you dim the lights at least one hour before going to bed and, as much as possible, turn off electronic devices and other lights in your bedroom (even the smallest light can lower your melatonin).

2. **Reduce exposure to blue light before bed.** If you do need to be exposed to lights in the evening, you can buy special orange-colored glasses that block blue light (emitted from computer screens and other electronic devices), as this type of light turns off melatonin production. Wearing these glasses can stop the blue light from being noticed by your brain. There are also software programs that lower the blue light exposure from your computer or other devices, while still allowing you to see the screen. You can find a few suggested brands in the "Recommended Third-Party Products" section at the back of this book.

3. **Take a melatonin supplement*.** You can take melatonin as a supplement to help increase your levels. It comes as capsules, liquids, sublingual lozenges (that dissolve under your tongue), and time-re-

leased. I usually recommend the capsule form. A common starting dose is 1 mg, taken within an hour of going to bed/sleep, optimally around 9 pm. If you don't see enough of a difference with 1 mg, you could increase to 2 or 3 mg. In some cases the dose may be increased to 5-20 mg, though I wouldn't advise doing this except on the advice of a qualified practitioner. You may also find that taking 1-5 mg of melatonin will help you adjust to a new time zone when traveling. I suggest taking the melatonin at bedtime (10 pm) in the new time zone. It is important to note that melatonin does not have addictive qualities or withdrawal symptoms, although it can cause you to sleep more deeply and your dreams to be more vivid.

4. **Check your serotonin levels.** Melatonin is made in the body from tryptophan and serotonin (with the help of vitamin B6), so if your melatonin is low, it's important to consider whether your serotonin is low, as well. Serotonin can be measured in a urine panel and, if levels are low, can be supported by taking a tryptophan or 5HTP supplement. As your serotonin levels increase, so will your melatonin levels.

5. **Manage your light exposure when you wake in the morning.** Research[40, 41] indicates that when we are exposed to light (blue light in particular) in the morning upon rising, it can help reset our circadian rhythm, leading to improved sleep.

* Please note that melatonin supplements may not be available in your country (the United Kingdom, for example). In most cases, you should be able to find a product that is a precursor to melatonin, which can help your brain produce more melatonin naturally.

You can also find products that contain a combination of melatonin and 5HTP ("Kavinace ULTRA" is one example), to optimize the amount of both serotonin and melatonin in your body. You can find a full list of products and tests in "Tests, Supplements and Where to Get Them" at the end of this book.

What Next?

Melatonin, like all hormones, delivers important messages throughout our bodies. When it is low – often due to exposure to stress and light at night – we are likely to experience the negative effects of not enough melatonin. It is such a valuable hormone – not only in terms of sleep, but also for healthy cells, immune function, and mood – that it's worth identifying whether it's an issue for you, and addressing it if it is.

If you follow these steps and find you *still* aren't sleeping, then it's time to dig deeper and get a better understanding of what is keeping you awake. Quite often it's more than one thing. It could be that you have low melatonin **and** elevated cortisol, for example.

Or perhaps it's a combination of leaky gut, food sensitivities, low serotonin and low melatonin, all of which are related to each other, but need to be addressed individually. Or inflammation (whether from an injury or a particularly food) may be disrupting your sleep, causing you to gain weight and further upsetting your sleep patterns.

To break these vicious cycles, we first need to understand all the causes, and then address each of them in turn. Once again, this process requires patience and diligence, which can be challenging when you're not sleeping at night. But trust the process! Over time, your body WILL start to adjust and your sleep will be restored.

CHAPTER 14

STRESS AND SLEEP PROBLEMS

A 2007 study[42] found that seven out of ten adults in the United States report experiencing stress daily, and 70% of those people have trouble sleeping. In turn, 75% said sleep problems increased their stress and anxiety.

This shows that insomnia is both **the cause** and **the result** of increased stress – the more stress you experience, the less sleep you get, and the less sleep you get, the more stressed you are.

The Connection Between Stress and Sleep

When we look more closely at stress, it becomes clear that the other 11 possible causes of sleep issues are either *caused by stress*, or they themselves are *a cause of stress*, which then disrupts your sleep.

I define stress as anything that triggers a *stress response* in the body and/or anything that causes the body to respond in an attempt to maintain a state of optimal health. By this definition, stress includes large and recurrent emotional/psychological triggers, as well as physical demands and imbalances in the body such as inflammation, hormone shifts and neurotransmitter fluctuations.

Therefore, everything including staying up late to study, being exposed to light that disrupts melatonin levels, and eating foods that cause a cascade of inflammatory messengers throughout the body are all stresses that have the potential to throw off your sleep. Even toxins in the air or environment are also a stress.

I simplify stress in this way because I find it is then easier to accept that we are all constantly exposed to stress, and that it's a matter of finding a balance and making choices that support our bodies when they are under pressure.

The main stress hormone itself, cortisol, has the potential to keep you up at night, or to make you feel that you can't get out of bed in the morning. However, we can make lifestyle choices that help bring our cortisol levels back to optimal. We can also take nutrients and herbs that help our adrenal glands produce the right quantity of cortisol throughout the day (more in the morning, gradually reducing through the day).

We each have a very unique response to stress that is partially determined by our genes, partly determined by our exposure to stress including as a child, and even our parent's exposure to stress. The important thing is to understand how your body responds to stress, and then give it the support it needs to stay healthy (and sleep) even when there is stress.

What to Do When Stress Keeps You Awake

- **Assess your stress.** First and foremost, it's vital to get to the root cause of what is causing you stress, and to understand how it is affecting your health. On my website, I have a free adrenal distress quiz that you can use as a preliminary self-assessment. If you want to go a bit deeper, I have a more comprehensive stress assessment in my book, The Stress Remedy, which can also tell you whether you need to be looking at leaky gut, blood sugar issues and/or adrenal distress.

- **Test your cortisol, adrenaline and neurotransmitter levels.** To take these tests, you'll need to see a naturopathic or functional practitioner who is familiar with the testing and will be able to assist you with interpreting and addressing the results. Neurotransmitter levels, in particular, are often missed, but they are key to understanding your sleep.

- **Test your hormone levels.** While completing a cortisol panel (at 4 different times of day), you may also need to check your melatonin levels, as well as estrogen and progesterone, and/or testosterone, to see if they are playing a role. This way, you'll have a full picture of how these hormones are influencing your sleep.

- **Get some blood tests.** Check your blood levels of thyroid-stimulating hormone, free T4, free T3, glucose, HgbA1c (average blood sugar), CRP (C reac-

129

tive protein), and nutrient levels such as vitamin D, magnesium (RBC magnesium), iron (ferritin), homocysteine methylmalonic acid (related to B6, B12 and folate. Nutrient deficiencies and/or blood sugar or hormone imbalances revealed in blood work can be addressed, thus benefitting your sleep.

- **Test for food sensitivities.** Next, do an IgG and IgA food panel if you haven't already, so you can find out if there are any foods that are playing a role in your sleep issues. You'll want to contact a naturopathic/ functional medicine practitioner, or you can order a kit here and complete it at home.

- **Do a genetic panel.** This can be done with a simple saliva collection. Then you take the data from that panel and put it into software programs that can tell you about your genetic predisposition, but also areas in your body that need more help. There are practitioners (like me and the practitioners I train) who know how to interpret genetic panels and provide dietary and nutrient suggestions based on that information.

- If oxidative stress, imbalanced bacteria in your digestive tract, and nutrient deficiencies could be a part of your case, then a **urine organic acid panel** will also be helpful. This type of test tells us about what is going on inside your cells and what kind of support they need in terms of nutrients. And if you suspect toxin or mold exposure, you'll want to have those levels checked as well.

- **Piece together the puzzle.** Putting all the pieces together is pretty complex, so you'll definitely want to do this with a practitioner who can help you prioritize and identify your first steps. It can be tempting to make many changes all at once, but that can be overwhelming, especially if you don't feel well. So keep the big picture in mind, but integrate the information bit by bit until it is working like a symphony for your health.

- **Don't give up.** If one nutrient or product trial doesn't go as expected, learn from it and move on to the next. Being hard on yourself and stopping yourself from trying again will only keep you where you are. It is patients who honor positive changes, and learn from setbacks, who achieve their goals the soonest.

- **Pay attention to your body.** Be aware of your body; learn how stress affects it and what works to help keep you in balance with stress. Good sleep is one of the best things we can do to help our bodies stand up to daily stress, which is why it's imperative you sort out anything that is causing you to have less than optimal sleep.

NOTE: To find out about the various tests mentioned, please refer to the Resources section of this book.

Getting You the Sleep You Need

In today's modern world, people frequently say they are "stressed." What few of them understand is that their stress is causing a physical imbalance with specific measurable influences in their bodies.

In fact, even to refer to our condition simply as "stress" minimizes what it is. Stress is not a "thing" we can simply switch on or off; it is something far more intricate.

As you have seen throughout this book, chronic stress is actually a syndrome – a collection of symptoms, triggered by a chain reaction of any number of underlying causes. Don't take stress lightly. But don't stress about it either! And most of all, don't feel guilty if you're unsuccessful at conquering it on your own. Meet with an experienced naturopathic doctor who will understand the metabolic complexities of stress and be able to work with you towards full recovery.

And again, try to not stress about not sleeping. If you catch yourself stressing about not sleeping, stop and find a way to reconnect with yourself. That could be breathing, listening to music, journaling, meditation, or doing yoga. When you are in a place of connecting with yourself, then you'll be more able to make choices to support your health and your recovery from stress.

You might also find that it is the processing of stress that wakes you in the night. If this is happening, you might wake from a nightmare or with your heart racing. Or you might

132

find yourself not wanting to go to bed, or waking unrested. If that is the case, it can help to work with a practitioner or therapist who specializes in processing stress and dreams. This way you can resolve the stress that is keeping you from getting good sleep.

The approach I have observed help the most with sleep by resetting our stress system, as well as decreasing inflammation, is Helminthic therapy. While for the longest time scientists emphasized the risks of having worms in our bodies, there are numerous studies over the past decade indicating that certain worms can actually help modulate our immune system and benefit our health. Since reading this research and finding a source for the most effective worms (hookworms), I gave myself a dose of hookworms and experienced the benefits myself. My allergies went away, and I've been sleeping better than ever. So I absolutely consider helminth or hookworm therapy to be an effective solution for insomnia. Most important is to work with a practitioner who can assure access to the best worms and guidance for the process.

CHAPTER 15

DR. DONI'S SLEEP RECOVERY PROTOCOL

When you've been struggling with poor health for a long time, you can sometimes wonder if you'll ever feel well again. I also know that, even when you've found a naturopathic doctor who can help you, the changes in diet and lifestyle you are being asked to make, and the learning curve of all the new information, can feel overwhelming.

So in this chapter, I break down the process of recovering with my three-part protocol: remove, restore, and resilience.

Step 1: Assess and Remove Stresses

As discussed in Chapter 14, "Stress" is not just a feeling or mental state; it's also a physical state. Your body becomes stressed when it cannot handle what is happening to it. Anything that puts your body in a state of stress is a "stressor."

Psychological stress, injury, infection, toxins, and trauma – all these kinds of stress will affect four main systems in our bodies: Digestion, immune system, nervous system, and hormones. When these systems become imbalanced, the can lead to three main health issues that can trap us in an ongoing state of poor health: Adrenal distress, intestinal permeability (leaky gut), and imbalanced metabolism (blood sugar issues).

Every one of us is exposed to stress/stressors every day; it is impossible to eliminate them altogether. However, some stressors – such as toxins or allergens in our air, food or water, or infections in our body – can trigger inflammation and dysfunction in our bodies, making us feel unwell in some way.

Taking an over-the-counter medication for sleep, for example, cannot "fix" the underlying problem related to stress. The only way to start the healing process is to eliminate (or at least minimize) our exposure to the stressors that are triggering our symptoms. Without first removing these stressors from our environment, we'll just end up going in circles, experiencing the same problems over and over. That's why we started this book by cleaning up your sleep environment.

Of course, if still not sleeping well, you won't necessarily know WHAT other stressesto address and remove simply by looking at your symptoms. The only way to know for sure is to get checked for food sensitivities, blood sugar and hormone imbalances, toxins, imbalanced gut bacteria, and infections.

Whenever I start working with a new patient, the first thing I usually do is discuss which specialty panels are available to help us identify what is most likely triggering negative health symptoms. The next step is to create a plan for removing those triggers from their environment.

Sometimes, this can require significant changes in the patient's diet and lifestyle. Also, if the exposure has been going on for a while, it may take some time for the effects of those changes to become noticeable. So be prepared to get support to eat differently and to stick with it consistently over time.

If tests show the presence of infection, a virus, or overgrowth of yeast and/or bacteria, it is also essential to take steps to address the infection before anything else, as it can put stress on the immune system and the entire body.

Most conventional medical doctors will prescribe antibiotics to address bacterial infections, and while in some situations they are necessary, they can compromise the digestive system and become a "stress" if used over and over. For that reason, my goal is to teach patients how to use natural remedies (like herbs and nutrients) to get rid of infections whenever possible.

After reading through this book, have you identified some stresses to address? Are there health panels you'd like to have done in order to find out about foods or imbalanced bacteria that may be adding to your stress?

Make a list now of how you'd like to get started with step 1 of the Sleep Recovery Protocol.

Step 2: Rebalance and Restore Optimal Levels

To perform as it is meant to, ALL your bodily systems – hormones, metabolism, digestion, nervous, adrenal, and immune system – need to be in balance. The reason stressors trigger ill health is that they create imbalances in these systems.

And because all these systems are interconnected, if one system gets out of balance, it can affect one or more of the others. If this imbalance is left unaddressed for a long time, it can create a snowball effect, resulting in a vicious cycle that continually creates greater imbalance.

If your body is caught in this vicious cycle of imbalance, eliminating the stressors from your environment probably won't be enough to restore health. The only way to do that is to restore balance to the systems that have gone off track.

We cannot begin addressing these imbalances without first knowing which systems are out of balance. Again, there are specialty panels to help us identify these. These panels are not often recommended or used in a convention medical office, but they are essential for finding the underlying causes and what is needed to restore balance.

When I work with patients in this phase, my goal is to balance hormone levels, blood sugar, cortisol levels, gut bacteria, nutrients, neurotransmitters, and antioxidants. And to heal leaky gut.

Once we know which systems need attention, restoring balance is often a two-step process. First, we would restore calming support in the body. For example, we would aim to lower cortisol levels if they are too high, or increase calming neurotransmitters, such as serotonin and GABA, if they are too low. We would also take steps to calm blood sugar fluctuations and reduce any inflammation in the body.

Once the body has "calmed down," we would start working on restoring natural stimulators like adrenaline and cortisol (if either is too low). These can help restore energy levels and mental focus.

It is essential to work on the calming support before introducing stimulating supplements, or you are likely to end up feeling worse. Refer back to earlier chapters for details on how to best to rebalance in each area.

Step 3: Maintain Resilience to Stress

Once you have restored balance to your body's systems, your next aim should be to help your body maintain that balance, no matter what stress/stressors it might face in the future. This is what we mean by "resilience."

Resilience is the ability to go out into the world and bounce back when faced with things that may have made you sick in the past. It means your adrenal response is optimal, which, in turn, helps optimize your digestion, immune function, hormones, and neurotransmitters. When we are resilient, we get sick less often and recover more quickly. We become less susceptible to infection, allergens, and sensitivities.

In other words, the ultimate goal of my proprietary system is to help you STAY well.

Our bodies CAN heal when they are given the support they need.

Our genes determine our health tendencies. Our unique genetic profiles explain why one person is more likely to develop allergies, while another is more prone to joint pain, autoimmunity or even insomnia. But it is our stress exposure that has the ability to turn on these genetic tendencies

Get to know your genetic tendencies, so you can see where your body is most likely to need support. Then, using the wisdom of naturopathic medicine, follow my three-step process to modify your stress exposure and support your body based on your unique genes. In this way, you will finally get to the root causes of your health issues and…

…change the course of your health story..

I hope I have helped make your journey back to wellness a little easier, and inspired you to get started. It doesn't matter what age you are. When you start supporting your health, your body will respond rapidly, as if it has been waiting for you to make these changes.

Getting Your Sleep Back on Track

As research shows that eight out of ten people don't get good sleep, it is likely that each of us will be affected by this issue at some time or another. Whether you're being woken by a baby or a full bladder, a hot flash or pain, blood sugar issues or noise outside your window, low melatonin and/or elevated cortisol, it all results in you not getting enough rest and recovery time, which leaves you susceptible to both immediate and long-term illness.

A high percentage of the patients I see have sleep issues, whether with not being able to fall to sleep, or with waking in the night or early morning. In frustration (or desperation), prior to coming to me, many have already resorted to over-the-counter medicines, prescription medication or even alcohol to help them sleep.

While some patients may find medications to be a temporary necessity, experience has shown me that making a concerted effort to understand and address the *underlying causes* of a patient's sleep issues is the only way to restore good sleep without medications.

Although each case has its own unique combination of causes, one of the most common situations I see is elevated cortisol and stimulating neurotransmitters at night, triggered by stress during the day as well as leaky gut, food sensitivities and an imbalance of intestinal bacteria.

Case after case, when we are able to decrease cortisol and adrenaline when elevated at night, while also re-optimizing calming neurotransmitters, and supporting the body to heal leaky gut and balance gut bacteria, sleep becomes easier and easier. Once that is achieved, our goal then becomes *preventing those imbalances from recurring.*

This requires many lifestyle and dietary changes (such as those we have explored throughout this book) that can finally rebalance our stress response and reduce stress on a daily basis.

To achieve that degree of improvement, and because the causes of sleep problems can be so complex, it can often be much more effective to work closely with an experienced naturopathic doctor who offers testing, guidance, and support with expert use of nutrients and herbs that bring the body back into balance.

So now, it's time for you to take back control of your sleep. Throughout this book, I have tried my best to give you enough information to get started on your own natural healing journey back to restful sleep. I have also included many resources and support at the back of this book to make that journey easier for you.

142

Wishing you a lifetime of restful slumber and sweet dreams!

~ Dr. Doni Wilson, N.D.

References

Chapter 1

1. Institute of Medicine. "Sleep disorders and sleep deprivation: an unmet public health problem." Washington, DC: *The National Academies Press*; 2006.

2. CDC. "Unhealthy sleep-related behaviors – 12 states, 2009." *MMWR* 2011; 60:233–238. Accessed February 19, 2015 from

http://www.cdc.gov/mmwr/preview/mmwrhtml/mm6008a2.htm

3. Ram S, Seirawan H, Kumar SK, Clark GT. "Prevalence and impact of sleep disorders and sleep habits in the United States." *Sleep Breath.* 2010;14:63–70

4. Wong, Manuck, DiNardo, Korytkowski and Muldoon. 2014. "Shorter Sleep Duration is Associated with Decreased Insulin Sensitivity in Healthy White Men." Retrieved 30 October 2014 from http://www.ncbi.nlm.nih.gov/pubmed/25325485.

5. Spira, Chen-Edinboro, Wu and Yaffe. 2014. "Impact of sleep on the risk of cognitive decline and dementia." Retrieved 30 October 2014 from

http://www.ncbi.nlm.nih.gov/pubmed/25188896.

Chapter 2

6. Marquezea, Lemosa, Soaresa, Lorenzi-Filhob and Morenoa. 2012. "Weight gain in relation to night work among nurses." Retrieved 30 October 2014 from

http://www.ncbi.nlm.nih.gov/pubmed/22317017.

7. Haus and Smolensky. 2013. "Shift work and cancer risk: potential mechanistic roles of circadian disruption, light at night, and sleep deprivation." Retrieved 30 October 2014 from

http://www.ncbi.nlm.nih.gov/pubmed/23137527.

8. Hamer and Smith. 2014. "Response: Influence of sleep disorders on television viewing time, diabetes and obesity." Retrieved 30 October 2014 from

http://www.ncbi.nlm.nih.gov/pubmed/25307739.

9. Exelmans and Van den Bulck. 2014. "The Use of Media as a Sleep Aid in Adults." Retrieved 30 October 2014 from

http://www.ncbi.nlm.nih.gov/pubmed/25313639.

10. Colbay, Cetin, Colbay, Berker and Guler. 2014. "Type 2 diabetes affects sleep quality by disrupting the respiratory function." Retrieved 30 October 2014 from

http://www.ncbi.nlm.nih.gov/pubmed/25266369.

11. Gonnissen, Mazuy, Rutters, Martens, Adam and Westerterp-Plantenga. 2013. "Sleep architecture when sleeping at an unusual circadian time and associations with insulin sensitivity." Retrieved 30 October 2014 from

http://www.ncbi.nlm.nih.gov/pubmed/23951335.

12. May and Mehra. 2014. "Obstructive sleep apnea: role of intermittent hypoxia and inflammation." Retrieved 30 October 2014 from

http://www.ncbi.nlm.nih.gov/pubmed/25333334.

13. Klöting and Blüher. 2014. "Adipocyte dysfunction, inflammation and metabolic syndrome." Retrieved 30 October 2014 from

http://www.ncbi.nlm.nih.gov/pubmed/25344447.

14. Zingone, Siniscalchi, Capone, Tortora, Andreozzi, Capone and Ciacci. 2010. "The quality of sleep in patients with coeliac disease." Retrieved 30 October 2014 from

http://www.ncbi.nlm.nih.gov/pubmed/20937049.

15. Daulatzai. 2014. "Chronic functional bowel syndrome enhances gut-brain axis dysfunction, neuroinflammation, cognitive impairment, and vulnerability to dementia." Retrieved 30 October 2014 from

http://www.ncbi.nlm.nih.gov/pubmed/24590859.

16. Moreno-Frías, Figueroa-Vega and Malacara. 2014. "Relationship of sleep alterations with perimenopausal and postmenopausal symptoms." Retrieved 30 October 2014 from

http://www.ncbi.nlm.nih.gov/pubmed/24569619.

17. Kolesnikova, Madaeva, Semenova, Suturina, Berdina, Sholohov and Solodova. 2013. "Pathogenic role of melatonin in sleep disorders in menopausal women." Retrieved 30 October 2014 from

http://www.ncbi.nlm.nih.gov/pubmed/24319702.

18. Magnusson Hanson, Chungkham, Akerstedt and Wester-lund. 2014. "The Role of Sleep Disturbances in the Longitudinal Relationship between Psychosocial Working Conditions, Measured by Work Demands and Support, and Depression." Retrieved 30 October 2014 from

http://www.ncbi.nlm.nih.gov/pubmed/25325503.

19. Michels, Sioen, Boone, Clays, Vanaelst, Huybrechts and De Henauw. 2014. "Cross-Lagged Associations between Children's Stress and Adiposity: The Children's Body Composition and Stress Study." Retrieved 30 October 2014 from

http://www.ncbi.nlm.nih.gov/pubmed/25341703.

Chapter 8

20. Leproult R, Van Cauter E. "Role of sleep and sleep loss in hormonal release and metabolism." *Endocr Dev*. 2010; 17:11-21.

21. Reutrakul S, Van Cauter E. "Interactions between sleep, circadian function, and glucose metabolism: implications for risk and severity of diabetes." *Ann N Y Acad Sci*. 2014 Apr; 1311:151-73.

22. Leproult R, Holmbäck U, Van Cauter E. "Circadian misalignment augments markers of insulin resistance and inflammation, independently of sleep loss.à *Diabetes*. 2014 Jun; 63(6):1860-9.

23. Zhang J, Lam SP, Li SX, Ma RC, Kong AP, Chan MH, Ho CS, Li AM, Wing YK. "A community-based study on the association between insomnia and hypothalamic-pitu-

itary-adrenal axis: sex and pubertal influences." *J Clin Endocrinol Metab.* 2014 Jun; 99(6):2277-87.

24. Arnardottir ES, Mackiewicz M, Gislason T, Teff KL, Pack AI. "Molecular signatures of obstructive sleep apnea in adults: a review and perspective." *Sleep.* 2009 Apr; 32(4):447-70.

Chapter 9

25. Maria Basta, M.D., George P Chrousos, M.D, Antonio Vela-Bueno, M.D, and Alexandros N Vgontzas, M.D. 2007. "Chronic Insomnia and Stress System." *Sleep Med Clin.* 2007 Jun; 2(2): 279–291.

http://www.ncbi.nlm.nih.gov/pmc/articles/PMC2128619/

26. Raison CL, Rye DB, Woolwine BJ, Vogt GJ, Bautista BM, Spivey JR, Miller AH. 2010. "Chronic interferon-alpha administration disrupts sleep continuity and depth in patients with hepatitis C: association with fatigue, motor slowing, and increased evening cortisol." *Biological Psychiatry.* 2010 Nov 15; 68(10): 942-9.

http://www.ncbi.nlm.nih.gov/pubmed/20537611

Chapter 10

27. Punder K, Pruimboom L. "The Dietary Intake of Wheat and other Cereal Grains and Their Role in Inflammation." *Nutrients.* 2013 March; 5(3): 771–787.

28. Fasano A. "Intestinal Permeability and its Regulation by Zonulin: Diagnostic and Therapeutic Implications." *Clin Gastroenterol Hepatol.* 2012 October; 10(10): 1096–1100.

29. Hadjivassiliou et al. "Gluten sensitivity as a neurological illness" *Journal of Neurology, Neurosurgery and Psychiatry.* 2002: 72:560-563.

Chapter 11

30. Marc DT, Ailts JW, Campeau DC, Bull MJ, Olson KL. "Neurotransmitters excreted in the urine as biomarkers of nervous system activity: validity and clinical applicability." *Neurosci Biobehav Rev.* 2011 Jan; 35(3):635-44.

31. Haroon E, Raison CL, Miller AH. "Psychoneuroimmunology Meets Neuropsychopharmacology: Translational Implications of the Impact of Inflammation on Behavior." *Neuropsychopharmacology.* 2012 January; 37(1): 137–162.

Chapter 13

32. Comai S, Ochoa-Sanchez R, Dominguez-Lopez S, Bambico FR, Gobbi G. "Melancholic-Like Behaviors and Circadian Neurobiological Abnormalities in Melatonin MT1 Receptor Knockout Mice." *International Journal of Neuropsychopharmacology.* 2015 Jan 31; 18(3).

pii: pyu075. doi: 10.1093/ijnp/pyu075.

33. Nagy AD, Iwamoto A, Kawai M, Goda R, Matsuo H, Otsuka T, Nagasawa M, Furuse M, Yasuo S. "Melatonin adjusts the expression pattern of clock genes in the suprachiasmatic nucleus and induces antidepressant-like effect in a mouse model of seasonal affective disorder." *Chronobiol Int.* 2014 Dec 17:1-11.

34. de Zanette SA, Vercelino R, Laste G, Rozisky JR, Schwertner A, Machado CB, Xavier F, de Souza IC, Deitos A, Torres IL, Caumo W1. "Melatonin analgesia is associated with improvement of the descending endogenous pain-modulating system in fibromyalgia: a phase II, randomized, double-dummy, controlled trial." *BMC Pharmacol Toxicol.* 2014 Jul 23; 15:40.

doi: 10.1186/2050-6511-15-40.

35. Neese R, Finch C, Nunn C. "Does selection for short sleep duration explain human vulnerability to Alzheimer's disease?" *Evol Med Public Health.* 2017; 2017(1): 39–46.

doi: 10.1093/emph/eow035.

36. Plaimee P, Weerapreeyakul N, Barusrux S, Johns NP. "Melatonin potentiates cisplatin-induced apoptosis and cell cycle arrest in human lung adenocarcinoma cells." *Cell Prolif.* 2015 Feb; 48(1):67-77.

37. Cos S, Alvarez-García V, González A, Alonso-González C, Martínez-Campa C. "Melatonin modulation of crosstalk among malignant epithelial, endothelial and adipose cells in breast cancer" (Review). *Oncol Lett.* 2014 Aug; 8(2):487-492.

38. Harb F1, Hidalgo MP, Martau B. "Lack of exposure to natural light in the workspace is associated with physiological, sleep and depressive symptoms." *Chronobiol* Int. 2014 Nov 26:1-8.

39. Chang AM, Aeschbach D, Duffy JF, Czeisler CA. "Evening use of light-emitting eReaders negatively affects sleep, circadian timing, and next-morning alertness." *Proc Natl Acad Sci U S A.* 2015 Jan 27; 112(4):1232-7.

doi: 10.1073/pnas.1418490112. Epub 2014 Dec 22.

40. Revell VL, Molina TA, Eastman CI. "Human phase response curve to intermittent blue light using a commercially available device." *Journal Physiol.* 2012 Oct 1; 590 (Pt 19):4859-68. doi: 10.1113/jphysiol.2012.235416. Epub 2012 Jul 2. Accessed 26 February 2015 from

http://www.ncbi.nlm.nih.gov/pubmed/22753544.

41. Burke TM, Markwald RR, Chinoy ED, Snider JA, Bessman SC, Jung CM, Wright KP Jr. "Combination of light and melatonin time cues for phase advancing the human circadian clock." *Sleep.* 2013 Nov 1;36 11):1617-24. doi: 10.5665/sleep.3110. Accessed 26 February 2015 from

http://www.ncbi.nlm.nih.gov/pubmed/24179293.

Chapter 14

42. Anxiety and Depression Society of America. 2007. "Stress and Anxiety Interfere with Sleep." Accessed 26 February 2015 from

http://www.adaa.org/understanding-anxiety/related-illnesses/other-related-conditions/stress/stress-and-anxiety-interfere

OTHER BOOKS BY DR. DONI WILSON

The Stress Remedy:
Master Your Body's Synergy and Optimize Your Health

By Dr. Doni Wilson. 340 pages:

http://doctordoni.com/stress-remedy

In The Stress Remedy, Dr. Wilson shows you:

- What stress REALLY is
- The science of how it affects the body
- How to calculate your own "stress score"
- How to determine which of your problem networks are out of balance
- How to measure cortisol and fix adrenal burn-out
- How to avoid environmental and dietary toxins
- How to rebalance and heal your body – and your life

In this book, you will learn:

- How virtually every health problem you experience can be traced back to the effects of stress on your body and mind

- Why missing meals and losing sleep can actually cause you to gain weight

- How your body's "stress messengers" can either disrupt your entire system or create a whole new level of energy and vitality

- Why the foods you choose can either boost your mood or send you spiraling into anxiety, fatigue, or depression

- How understanding blood-sugar imbalance can free you from weight gain and a host of other symptoms

- Why just 5 minutes a day of doing something you love can make a revolutionary difference to your health

PLUS to make your wellness journey even easier (and tastier!) The Stress Remedy also contains **50 pages of recipes** – all gluten, egg, dairy and soy FREE – that are all suitable for vegans, vegetarians and non-vegetarians. You'll also have a 3-week meal plan and tips on living a gluten-free life.

Stress Remedies:
How to Reduce Stress and Boost Your Health in Just 15 Minutes a Day

http://doctordoni.com/dr-donis-new-kindle-ebook-stress-remedies-just-99-cents

In this practical companion guide to her widely acclaimed book The Stress Remedy: Master Your Body's Synergy and Optimize Your Health, Dr. Doni starts by asking you the question, 'Has Stress Thrown Your Health Off Track?'

To help you answer that question, she will teach you all about the biology of stress, why it's so hard to switch it off, and how stress can be a doubled-edged sword when it comes to health.

Then, she'll guide you through a short quiz to help determine how much stress might be disrupting your health and overall quality of life.

Once you have a good picture of your own stress levels, Dr. Doni will show you how to rebalance your stress response in just 15 minutes, using five easy and effective stress remedies that cost you nothing, and involve no drugs or supplements.

Stress Warrior:

DOUBLE YOUR ENERGY, FOCUS AND PRODUCTIVITY WHILE YOU DROP WEIGHT, BLOOD SUGAR, PAIN AND ANXIETY BY RECOVERING FROM LEAKY GUT, OXIDATIVE STRESS AND ADRENAL FATIGUE

StressWarriorBook.com

Reverse engineer your health and get your energy, focus, mood and optimal weight back by following this three-step approach to becoming a warrior to stress. Stress is a part of life. In this book you'll learn how to become resilient to stress so it doesn't wreck your business and life.

ARTICLES BY DR. DONI WILSON

The following articles by Dr. Doni address many of the subjects discussed throughout this book.

Stress, Adrenals and Cortisol

Wilson, Dr. Doni. 2009. "It All Starts with Stress."

http://doctordoni.com/ItAllStartsWithStress.pdf

Wilson, Dr. Doni. 2014. "5 Signs that Your Stress Response is Out of Balance."

http://doctordoni.com/2014/05/five-signs-that-your-stress-response-is-out-of-balance.html

Wilson, Dr. Doni. 2014. "Adrenal Distress: How to Take Action."

http://doctordoni.com/2014/08/adrenal-distress-how-to-take-action.html

Wilson, Dr. Doni. 2014. "What is Adrenal Burn-out?"

http://doctordoni.com/2014/07/what-is-adrenal-burn-out.html

Wilson, Dr. Doni. 2014. "The 3 Problem Networks of Stress."

http://doctordoni.com/2014/07/3-problem-networks-of-stress.html

Wilson, Dr. Doni. 2018. "Adrenal Recovery: Are You Giving Your Body Everything it Needs?"

https://doctordoni.com/2018/02/adrenal-recovery/

Wilson, Dr. Doni. 2018. "What is a Stress Warrior?"

https://doctordoni.com/2018/07/what-is-a-stress-warrior/

Sugar, Blood Sugar, Protein and Healthy Fats

Wilson, Dr. Doni. 2014. "How Sugar – Not Fat – Raises Your Cholesterol."

http://doctordoni.com/2014/03/how-sugar-not-fat-raises-your-cholesterol.html

Wilson, Dr. Doni. 2014. "The Sugar Challenge: Cut it Out and Change Your Life."

https://doctordoni.com/2014/09/the-sugar-challenge/

Wilson, Dr. Doni. 2014. "Carbohydrates, Blood Sugar and Your Health."

https://doctordoni.com/2014/08/carbohydrates-blood-sugar-and-your-health/

Wilson, Dr. Doni. 2017. "Protein Powder: A Beginner's Guide."

https://doctordoni.com/2017/02/protein-powder-beginners-guide/

Wilson, Dr. Doni. 2017. "Why Eating Good Fat Keeps You Slim, Happy and Healthy."

https://doctordoni.com/2017/04/eating-good-fat/

Leaky Gut, Gluten and Food Sensitivities

Wilson, Dr. Doni. 2014. "5 Clues that Leaky Gut May Be at the Root of Your Health Issues."

http://doctordoni.com/2014/08/5-clues-that-leaky-gut-may-be-at-the-root-of-your-health-issues.html

Wilson, Dr. Doni. 2014. "Three Ways to Tell if You Have a Gluten Sensitivity."

http://doctordoni.com/2014/05/three-ways-to-tell-if-you-have-a-gluten-sensitivity.html

Wilson, Dr. Doni. 2009. "Starting Out on a Gluten Free Quest."

http://doctordoni.com/2009/10/starting-out-on-a-gluten-free-quest.html

Wilson, Dr. Doni. 2017. " Leaky Gut, MTHFR, and How to Fix It."

https://doctordoni.com/2017/10/leaky-gut-mthfr-and-how-to-fix-it/

Inflammation and Liver Function

Wilson, Dr. Doni. 2014. "Inflammation is at the Core of Most, if Not All, Health Issues."

http://doctordoni.com/2014/03/inflammation-is-at-the-core-of-most-health-issues.html

Wilson, Dr. Doni. 2017. "Inflammation and MTHFR: How to Recover Without Medication."

https://doctordoni.com/2017/10/mthfr-and-inflammation/

Wilson, Dr. Doni. 2017. "How Liver Function and MTHFR Relate to Sugar and Alcohol Consumption."

https://doctordoni.com/2017/11/liver-function-and-mthfr/

MTHFR and Genetics

Wilson, Dr. Doni. 2014. "Folic Acid and MTHFR – Could You Have a Genetic Mutation?"

http://doctordoni.com/2014/04/folic-acid-and-mthfr-could-you-have-a-genetic-mutation.html

Wilson, Dr. Doni. 2016. "Your Health is Not Set in Stone: Your Genetics and You." https://doctordoni.com/2016/08/your-health-is-not-set-in-stone-your-genetics-and-you/

Wilson, Dr. Doni. 2017. "I Have an MTHFR Mutation: What Do I Do Now?"

https://doctordoni.com/2017/08/i-have-an-mthfr-mutation/

Wilson, Dr. Doni. 2017. " MTHFR: 4 Things to Consider Before Taking Folate."

https://doctordoni.com/2017/12/taking-folate-with-mthfr/

Wilson, Dr. Doni. 2017. "How Adrenal Distress Affects MTHFR and Methylation."

https://doctordoni.com/2017/09/how-adrenal-distress-affects-mthfr-and-methylation/

Oxidative Stress

Wilson, Dr. Doni. 2014. "5 Signs of Oxidative Stress."

http://doctordoni.com/2014/10/5-signs-of-oxidative-stress.html

Wilson, Dr. Doni. 2016. "Oxidative Stress: What is it and How can it Affect Your Health?"

https://doctordoni.com/2015/11/oxidative-stress-what-is-it-and-how-can-it-affect-your-health/

Wilson, Dr. Doni. 2016. "SOS! Stress, Oxidative Stress and Sleep."

https://doctordoni.com/2016/04/sos-stress-oxidative-stress-and-sleep/

Wilson, Dr. Doni. 2017. "What Causes Oxidative Stress + How to Reverse It."

https://doctordoni.com/2017/12/what-causes-oxidative-stress/

Tests, Health Panels, Supplements and Where to Get Them

The following tests and supplements are all offered by Dr. Doni. If they are available via her online store, you will find the links to them below. Alternatively, you can search for them by name by going to Dr. Doni's online store at DrDoniStore.com.

To review the services Dr. Doni offers, including her Natural Sleep Solutions Program and Dr. Doni's High Performance System, as well as her group and online programs, visit https://doctordoni.com/work-with-dr-doni/. From there you'll be able to apply to work with her one-on-one or with one of her associates.

Tests and Health Panels

Blood work

The blood work mentioned in this book can be ordered directly and paid out of pocket (not billed to insurance) at YourLabWork.com and/or UltaLabs.

IgG and IgA Food Panel

An IgG and IgA food panel can help you determine whether or not you have delayed food sensitivities, and which foods you might be sensitive to. Done with a finger-prick blood sample, you can do this test at home and send it to the laboratory through the mail. The lab with check your sample against 96 of the most common foods, including gluten and dairy, to find out if your immune system is attacking the food you are eating. You can order this test through your naturopathic doctor or from Dr. Doni at:

- IgG and IgA Food Sensitivity Home Testing

https://www.drdonistore.com/IgG-IgA-Food-Sensitivity-Home-Testing_p_262.html

Estrogen, progesterone and testosterone levels

While these hormones can be measured in blood, saliva or urine, Dr. Doni's preference at this point in time, and for the purpose of understanding the hormone levels and metabolism, is the dried urine test from Precision Analytical (DUTCH test). This panel is able to show how much estrogen and progesterone is being metabolized and how well estrogen is being metabolized. The dried urine test is also an effective way to evaluate estrogen and progesterone levels even when taking hormones. A practitioner with training in the use of these tests will be able to tell you if testing is right for you and, if so, which test will be most helpful. Ask your naturopathic doctor or Dr. Doni about arranging to do this test.

Cortisol, DHEA, and melatonin

A saliva or urine panel can be used to measure cortisol, DHEA, and melatonin. Precision Analytical can run these hormones along with estrogen, progesterone and testosterone as described above.

For cortisol, it is best to collect four timed samples, which are usually collected upon waking, mid-day, evening, bedtime. In cases where you are waking in the middle of the night, collecting a saliva or urine sample at that time can be helpful as well. Melatonin is most often measured at 10 pm when it should be at the highest level. In some cases it will also be measured in the night upon waking and/or other times of day, especially if you work the night shift.

If you are interested in these tests, ask your naturopathic doctor or contact Dr. Doni's office at DrDoni.com.

Neurotransmitter levels

Urine can be used to measure adrenaline levels as well as neurotransmitters such as serotonin, GABA, glutamate, dopamine, norepinephrine and epinephrine. In most cases the second morning urine is collected. If you are waking in the night, a urine sample at the time of waking can be useful. At this time, Dr. Doni recommends Sanesco NeuroLab.

A practitioner with training in the use of these panels will be able to tell you if testing is right for you and, if so, which test will be most helpful. Ask your naturopathic doctor or Dr. Doni's office to arrange this type of panel.

Specialty Stool Panel

There are several available that Dr. Doni feels it is important to get the most up to date stool panel, including a genetic analysis of the microbiome. These panels will all assess for commensal and pathogenic bacteria, parasites and protozoa, and yeast. Additional options are to check for zonulin levels, secretory IgA and inflammatory markers, as well as ability to digest foods and fat. You'll want to work with a practitioner to help you interpret and act on the results.

Organic Acids, Oxidative Stress, Toxins and Mold Toxins

Great Plains Lab is Dr. Doni's preferred lab for checking organic acids and toxin panels. These are urine tests that provide information about imbalanced gut bacteria, mitochondrial function, nutrient levels, and other metabolites that influence sleep. Evaluating for toxins is an important consideration when it comes to insomnia and other health issues.

Genetic Panel

There are several genetic panels to choose from that check common gene SNPS, such as MTHFR.

Toolbox Genomics

Ancestry.com combined with StrateGene

NOTE: If you are interested in meeting with Dr. Doni to have her help with any of these tests, you can learn about her services at DrDoni.com. Then, once the results come in, you'll be able to consult with her to discuss your results. She can also advise you on dietary changes and suggest supplements that may help.

Protein Shakes and Supplements

Protein Shakes

- Dr. Doni's Pea Protein, comes in Chocolate, Vanilla, Berry. *It contains 16 grams of protein per scoop plus nutrients, including methylfolate, and is sweetened with stevia.*

https://www.drdonistore.com/Dr-Donis-Pea-Protein-Shake_p_733.html

- Samples of Dr. Doni's Pea Protein *are available for free (with the cost of shipping), so you can try it out and see if you like it.*

https://www.drdonistore.com/Dr-Donis-Pea-Protein-Shake-Samples_p_792.html

- Plain Organic Pea Protein *is a very good option for those who have more severe leaky gut and need to keep things simple, and for those who prefer protein powder without stevia.*

https://www.drdonistore.com/Organic-PurePea-Protein-UnflavoredUnsweetened-450-g_p_864.html

- Innate Vegan Protein *is pea protein with vanilla, cinnamon and stevia.*

https://www.drdonistore.com/Vegan-Protein-Vanilla-169-oz_p_550.html

- Vital Proteins Collagen *comes in marine and beef versions and contains 11 grams of protein in 2 scoops.*

https://www.drdonistore.com/Collagen-Peptides-10-oz_p_780.html

- DFH Chocolate Collagen contains *beef collagen, with cocoa, stevia.*

https://www.drdonistore.com/PurePaleo-Protein-Chocolate-810-grams_p_914.html

Balance Blood Sugar and Optimize Insulin Function

- Metabolic Xtra *contains chromium and berberine, two substances know to support insulin function and stabilize blood sugar levels.*

https://www.drdonistore.com/Metabolic-Xtra-90-capsules_p_263.html

- *Cinnamon and other herbs and nutrients that help with blood sugar regulation can be found in combination products, such as* Blood Sugar Support.

https://www.drdonistore.com/Blood-Sugar-Support-120-Vegetarian-Capsules_p_498.html

Increase GABA

- One option is to take actual GABA, such as in **Calming Support by Dr. Doni**:

https://www.drdonistore.com/Dr-Donis-Calming-Support-90-capsules_p_980.html

- 4-amino-3-phenylbutyric acid is a precursor nutrient to GABA and is used to increase the production of GABA. Example product is **Kavinace**:

https://www.drdonistore.com/Kavinace_p_424.html

168

- Combining phenyl-butyric acid, melatonin and 5-HTP (the precursor to serotonin) is indicated when GABA, serotonin and melatonin all need support. If your naturopathic doctor determines that you could use serotonin and melatonin support, you might consider **Kavinace Ultra:**

https://www.drdonistore.com/Kavinace-Ultra-PM-30-capsules_p_212.html

- **Dr. Doni's Sleep Support** contains GABA, L-Theanine, along with melatonin, 5HTP (serotonin support), vitamin B6 and several calming herbs, including Passion Flower, Lemon Balm, Chamomile and Valerian.

https://www.drdonistore.com/Dr-Donis-Sleep-Support-60-capsules_p_979.html

Increase Serotonin

- 5-HTP is the precursor nutrient to serotonin. Example products are **Serene:**

https://www.drdonistore.com/Serene-60-capsules_p_384.html

and

5HTP by Prothera: https://www.drdonistore.com/5-HTP-100-mg-100-capsules_p_773.html

- Nutrients to support the production of serotonin include vitamin B6, B12, folate, zinc and 5HTP. An example product is **TravaCor:**

https://www.drdonistore.com/Travacor_p_456.html

- Tryptophan is a precursor to serotonin. It is first converted to 5HTP then to serotonin. An example product is:

https://www.drdonistore.com/L-Tryptophan-60-capsules_p_585.html

- **Dr. Doni's Sleep Support** contains GABA, L-Theanine, along with melatonin, 5HTP (serotonin support), vitamin B6 and several calming herbs, including Passion Flower, Lemon Balm, Chamomile and Valerian.

https://www.drdonistore.com/Dr-Donis-Sleep-Support-60-capsules_p_979.html

Decrease Glutamate

- L-theanine, CoQ10 and N-AcetylCysteine all help to decrease glutamate when it is too high. An example product containing all three is **Calm G**:

https://www.drdonistore.com/Calm-G-90-capsules_p_217.html

- **Dr. Doni's Sleep Support** contains GABA (which counterbalances GABA), L-Theanine, along with melatonin, 5HTP (serotonin support), vitamin B6 and several calming herbs, including Passion Flower, Lemon Balm, Chamomile and Valerian.

https://www.drdonistore.com/Dr-Donis-Sleep-Support-60-capsules_p_979.html

Decrease Cortisol

- Phosphatidylserine is a nutrient known to help get the brain out of stress mode and decrease cortisol. An example product is PS Plus:

https://www.drdonistore.com/PS-Plus-60-capsules_p_1055.html

- Banaba leaf and phosphatidylserine work in combination to help decrease cortisol when it is too high. An example product is **Calm CP:**

https://www.drdonistore.com/Calm-CP-60-capsules_p_215.html

- Ashwagandha root and phosphatidylserine all help to decrease cortisol. An example product is **Stress Support:**

https://www.drdonistore.com/Dr-Donis-Stress-Support-90-capsules_p_981.html

- Magnolia bark and Ziziphus are also known to decrease cortisol levels that are too high. **Seditol** contains these two herbs:

https://www.drdonistore.com/Seditol-60-capsules_p_761.html

Decrease Norepinephrine (aka adrenaline)

- Magnesium and vitamin B6 help process norepinephrine to epinephrine, essentially decreasing adrenaline levels. An example is **Magnesium Plus**:

https://www.drdonistore.com/Magnesium-Plus-100-vegetarian-capsules_p_35.html

- **Stress Support by Dr. Doni** contains B6 and magnesium to decrease adrenaline, along with ingredients to decrease cortisol, and calming herbs:

https://www.drdonistore.com/Dr-Donis-Stress-Support-90-capsules_p_981.html

- High concentrations of the herb rhodiola helps to decrease cortisol and adrenaline levels. One example of a supplement containing a high concentration of rhodiola is **Calm PRT:**

https://www.drdonistore.com/Calm-PRT_p_428.html

Calm nervous system (overall)

Herbs that are calming to the nervous system include valerian, chamomile, passionflower, hops and California poppy.

- One example product is **Sweet Dreams** herbal tincture:

https://www.drdonistore.com/Sweet-Dreams-2-oz_p_419.html

- **Dr. Doni's Sleep Support** contains GABA, L-Theanine, along with melatonin, 5HTP (serotonin support), vitamin B6 and several calming herbs, including Passion Flower, Lemon Balm, Chamomile and Valerian.

https://www.drdonistore.com/Dr-Donis-Sleep-Support-60-capsules_p_979.html

- **Hemp oil contains cannabinoids** which have been shown to help calming the nervous system and with stress recovery in general. Here are two example products: Hemp oil that is organic and CO2 extracted:

https://www.drdonistore.com/Hemp-Oil-30-capsules_p_1061.html

and

CannabOmega (with fish oil): https://www.drdonistore.com/CannabOmega-60-softgels_p_1012.html

Nutrients that calm the nervous system include **magnesium, B6, theanine** and **glycine.**

- Glycine can be found in both **Calm CP** and **Calming Support** *(see above),* as well as **Sleep Reset™ sachets** *(see description under "melatonin" below).*

- Magnesium and B6 can be found in **Stress Support by Dr. Doni and in Magnesium Plus.** See above for descriptions of these products.

- Magnesium threonate, which is particularly calming to the nervous system, is found in **NeuroMag**:

https://www.drdonistore.com/NeuroMag-90-vegetarian-capsules_p_896.html

- **Dr. Doni's Sleep Support** contains GABA, L-Theanine, along with melatonin, 5HTP (serotonin support), vitamin B6 and several calming herbs, including Passion Flower, Lemon Balm, Chamomile and Valerian.

https://www.drdonistore.com/Dr-Donis-Sleep-Support-60-capsules_p_979.html

Melatonin support

Melatonin increases at night when the lights are out and you are sleeping. If you are exposed to light at night, have a low melatonin level, and/or change time zones with travel and need to reset your sleep cycle, you might consider a melatonin supplement. Example products include:

- **Melatonin 3 mg:**

https://www.drdonistore.com/Melatonin-3-mg-60-caps_p_390.html

- **Melatonin-SR 2 mg:**

https://www.drdonistore.com/Melatonin-SR-2-mg-60-capsules_p_417.html

There are also many products that combine melatonin with other sleep support ingredients. Examples of these include:

- **Dr. Doni's Sleep Support** contains GABA, L-Theanine, along with melatonin, 5HTP (serotonin support), vitamin B6 and several calming herbs, including Passion Flower, Lemon Balm, Chamomile and Valerian.

https://www.drdonistore.com/Dr-Donis-Sleep-Support-60-capsules_p_979.html

- **ProThrivers Wellness Sleep** has melatonin with theanine, magnesium, and Magnolia (to lower cortisol):

https://www.drdonistore.com/ProThrivers-Wellness-Sleep_p_463.html

- **Kavinace ULTRA** contains 5HTP, phenylbutyric acid and melatonin:

https://www.drdonistore.com/Kavinace-Ultra-PM-30-capsules_p_212.html

- **Sleep Reset™ sachets** contain melatonin with turmeric (anti-inflammatory), 5HTP (serotonin support), theanine (decreases glutamate), glycine, and vitamin B6:

https://www.drdonistore.com/Sleep-Reset-Orange-Flavor--Restful-Sleep-Blend_p_462.html

Increase Cortisol

Herbs that support adrenal function and cortisol levels are referred to as "adaptogens." Rhodiola is an adaptogen that functions differently at different doses. Low doses of rhodiola can help increase cortisol when it is too low. There are many products that contain rhodiola in combination with other cortisol balancing nutrients and herbs. Some example products are:

- Dr. Doni's **Adrenal Support**: Contains tyrosine to support adrenaline, plus herbs and nutrients to support adrenal function and cortisol production, such as vitamin C, pantothenic acid, Eleutherococcus and Glycyrrhiza (herbal licorice).

https://www.drdonistore.com/Dr-Donis-Adrenal-Support-90-capsules_p_978.html

- **Adrenal Response**: A combination of vitamin C, pantothenate, magnesium, ashwagandha, L-serine, rhodiola extract, holy basil (tulsi) leaf, Cordyceps mushroom mycelia, Reishi mushroom, organic astragulus root, Schizandra, and other active ingredients.

- **Adrenal SAP licorice-free:** A combination of vitamins C, B6 and B5, plus magnesium, zinc, ashwagandha, holy basil (tulsi), Panax ginseng, Siberian ginseng, Schizandra, and astralagus.

- **AdreCor:** Contains the B vitamins, plus vitamin C, tyrosine, and herbs such as Rhodiola and green tea. These have all been shown to restore healthy adrenal function.

https://www.drdonistore.com/AdreCor_p_580.html

- **AdreCor with Licorice:** In addition to the standard AdreCor formula, this product contains licorice extract, which is known to significantly support cortisol levels.

https://www.drdonistore.com/AdreCor-with-Licorice-Root-90-capsules_p_360.html

- **AdreCor with SAMe:** In additional to the standard AdreCor formula, this product contains SAMe, which helps with the conversion from norepinephrine to epinephrine, resulting in healthier adrenaline and energy levels.

https://www.drdonistore.com/AdreCor-with-SAMe-30-capsules_p_361.html

Increase Norepinephrine (aka adrenaline)

Phenylalanine and tyrosine are precursor nutrients to norepinephrine, so if we need to increase the levels of norepinephrine, we can use those nutrients. Norepinephrine is made in part by the adrenal glands, so we can also increase norepinephrine levels by supporting adrenal gland function using herbs and/or nutrients, such as B vitamins (including pantothenic acid), vitamin C, and eleuthrococcus, glycyrrhiza, and rhodiola. Some suggested products are:

- **Adrenal Support by Dr. Doni:**

https://www.drdonistore.com/Dr-Donis-Adrenal-Support-90-capsules_p_978.html

- **AdreCor** *(see description above)*:

https://www.drdonistore.com/AdreCor_p_580.html

Liver – Detoxification of Estrogens

- **B vitamins** (B6/P5P, folate/5MTHF and B12) are needed by the liver to detoxify estrogens. An example product is **Methyl-Guard Plus:**

https://www.drdonistore.com/Methyl-Guard-Plus-90-capsules_p_367.html

- **Methylation** is an important step in the detoxification of estrogens. Choline provides methyl groups for that process. An example product is **Optimal PC:**

https://www.drdonistore.com/Optimal-PC-100-Softgels_p_28.html

- **DIM (diindolmethionine**) is a substance from broccoli that supports healthy estrogen metabolism. An example product containing the first and only stable bioavailable form of DIM by DFH:

https://www.drdonistore.com/DIM-Evail_p_666.html

- **Sulforaphane glucosinolate (SGS)** is a natural substance derived from the seeds and sprouts of broccoli that is an advanced antioxidant and has chemoprotective properties. An example product is **Crucera-SGS:**

https://www.drdonistore.com/Crucera-SGS-60-vegetarian-capsules_p_413.html

- **DIM with CDG:**

https://www.drdonistore.com/CDG-EstroDIM-60-capsules_p_710.html

177

- ### DIM with CDG and Broccoli:

https://www.drdonistore.com/DIM-with-Calcium-D-Glucarate-60-capsules_p_965.html

- **Curcumin** has been shown in research to support liver detoxification and decrease inflammation. An example product containing curcumin is **Meriva 500:**

https://www.drdonistore.com/Meriva-500-Soy-Free-120-capsules_p_758.html

- **Milk Thistle (Silymarin)** is supportive of liver detoxification including the production of glutathione. It is also known to assist the body in ridding itself of excess estrogens. Dr. Doni carries a 500 milligram milk thistle supplement at

https://www.drdonistore.com/Milk-Thistle-500-mg-120-veggie-capsules_p_309.html

- **Green Tea Extract (EGCF)** has been shown to help detoxify toxins and estrogens from the body, and decrease the negative effects of excess estrogen. An example product containing highly absorbed green tea is **Green Tea Phytosome:**

https://www.drdonistore.com/Green-Tea-Phytosome-60-capsules_p_350.html

Estrogen Support

- **Black Cohosh** (Cimicifuga) is an herb that assists with hot flashes, night sweats and other perimenopausal symptoms. It has been shown to be safe for patients who have, or who have had, breast cancer. An example product is **Black Cohosh** by Vitanica:

https://www.drdonistore.com/Black-Cohosh_p_500.html

- **Maca** is an herb that has been researched to help with PMS, perimenopausal and post-menopausal symptoms. It helps balance hormones and supports estrogen levels that are too low. An example product is called **Femmenessence**: For Peri-menopause;

https://www.drdonistore.com/Femmenessence-PRO-PERI-180-vegetarian-capsules_p_53.html

For Post-menopause:

https://www.drdonistore.com/Femmenessence-PRO-POST-180-vegetarian-capsules_p_172.html

Progesterone Support

- **Chaste tree berry (Vitex)** is an herb that supports the ovaries to ovulate and produce hormones on their own. It assists with the communication from the brain to the ovaries, resulting in increased progesterone production by the ovaries. An example product with high effectiveness is **Chaste Tree Berry by Vitanica**:

https://www.drdonistore.com/Chaste-Tree-Berry-60-capsules_p_166.html

- **Wild Yam (Dioscorea villosa)** acts as a mild progesterone-like substance in the body. It is available in both oral and topical (cream) forms. An example wild yam **cream** is available at

https://www.drdonistore.com/Dioscorea-Cream-56-gms_p_426.htmlIf

you prefer capsules, you can find them at

https://www.drdonistore.com/Dioscorea-Capsules-60-vegetarian-capsules_p_427.html

- **Progesterone cream** is derived from plant sources and can be applied topically as a way to support low progesterone levels. One example of a paraben-free cream is **Natural Progeste Cream** at

https://www.drdonistore.com/Natural-Progeste-Cream-35-oz_p_538.html

- **Adrenal support** can support healthy ovarian function and greatly improve perimenopausal and post-menopausal symptoms. One example of such a product is Dr. Doni's Adrenal Support

https://www.drdonistore.com/Dr-Donis-Adrenal-Support-90-capsules_p_978.html

Decrease Inflammation

- Herb that promote a healthy inflammation response include curcumin (from turmeric), skullcap, and rosemary. Phytocannabinoids from hemp oil (as well as cloves, black pepper, hops and rosemary) are known to decrease inflammation. Omega 3 (fish oils) also decrease inflammation. Bromelain is an enzyme known to decrease inflammation. Example products with these ingredients are:

- **Meriva 500:**

https://www.drdonistore.com/Meriva-500-Soy-Free-120-capsules_p_758.html

- **InflaCalm:**

https://www.drdonistore.com/InflaCalm-SAP-90-capsules_p_807.html

- **Zyflamend:**

https://www.drdonistore.com/Zyflamend-120-Vegetarian-Capsules_p_66.html

- Hemp oil that is organic and CO2 extracted:

https://www.drdonistore.com/Hemp-Oil-30-capsules_p_1061.html

- CannabOmega is hemp oil combined with fish oil:

https://www.drdonistore.com/CannabOmega-60-softgels_p_1012.html

- Omega 3 fish oil in a concentrated form and highest quality, that has been independently tests for metals and toxins is **Ultra Pure Fish Oil**:

https://www.drdonistore.com/Ultra-Pure-Fish-Oil-800-Triglyceride-90-gels_p_44.html

Leaky Gut Healing Support

- **Leaky Gut Support:**

https://www.drdonistore.com/Dr-Donis-Leaky-Gut-Support-61-oz_p_681.html

- **Enzyme Support:**

https://www.drdonistore.com/-Dr-Donis-Enzyme-Support-90-capsules_p_977.html

- **Probiotic Support:**

https://www.drdonistore.com/Dr-Donis-Probiotic-Support-60-vegetarian-capsules_p_271.html

Recommended Third-Party Products and Resources

Dr. Doni compiled sleep supportive products and resources for you here. She does not sell these products or guarantee them. They are listed here because either she or her clients have used them successfully.

Organic Mattress

Samina.com

Each layer of the system, including the natural mattress, was specifically designed to support something the human body needs while sleeping – this is the SAMINA Healthy Sleep Concept. The system works with your body and each layer works synergistically to ensure you fall asleep easy, you stay asleep and reducing or eliminating reasons your bed may cause you to toss and turn or awaken like you're too sweaty, hot or cold, and that you awaken refreshed. From the orthopedic flexible slat frame to the orthopedic pillows, the SAMINA Sleep System contours to each person's individual shape and size.

Air Filters

Recommended companies that manufacture high-quality air filters:

IQAIR - https://www.iqair.com

AlenCorp - https://www.alencorp.com

Austin Air - https://austinair.com

Air Doctor - https://www.airdoctorpro.com

Products to Cool Temperature in Bed

To keep your bed cool, you might wish to check out:

ChiliPad – https://www.chilitechnology.com

Cool Gel Pad – http://www.dreamproducts.com/forever-cool-gel-pad.html

Blue Light Blocking Glasses

True Dark Truedark.com

Blue light blocking glasses can also be found on Amazon from several companies. Check my Amazon page for products I like and recommend.

Free downloadable software f.lux makes the color of your computer's display adapt to the time of day, warm at night and like sunlight during the day.

Gluten-free and Dairy-free Meal Planning and Foods

PrepDish www.prepdish.com/drdoni

No more thinking. No more stress. No more meal time guesswork. With our Gluten Free and Paleo meal plans, you'll enjoy healthy, tasty meals with your family all week long! Receive real-food meal plans via email (you get BOTH gluten free & Paleo plans!). $10 off the premium subscription with code DrDoni.

PaleoTreats https://www.paleotreats.com/drdoni

We've been making foodie-approved Paleo desserts since 2009. We are serious about flavor, texture, ingredients and Paleo. Yes, all of them. We've shipped around the world, from Australia to Afghanistan, and we've ironed out all the kinks of getting a great dessert to your door. Get 10% off with the code DrDoni.

Find more foods and products Dr. Doni suggests on her Amazon page.

Meditation Online Training

ZivaMeditation.com

In only 2 weeks, you can reduce the stress in your body so you can perform at the top of your game. This isn't another challenge, zivaONLINE is a proven, in-depth training that will give you the most powerful meditation practice available. You'll get a powerful combination of: Meditation, mindfulness and manifesting.

Exercise Online Program

Flipping50.com/drdoni

Debra shows you how to integrate in fun and easy ways so you can reach your fitness goals

Non-Toxic Skincare

TheSpaDr.com

Toxin-free skin care products designed by a naturopathic doctor, Dr. Trevor Cates.

DR. DONI'S 21-DAY STRESS REMEDY PROGRAM

What is Dr. Doni's Stress Remedy Program?

Dr. Doni's Stress Remedy Program is a self-guided 21-day program, specially designed to:

- Support for implementing CARE: Clean Eating, Adequate Sleep, Reducing Stress and Exercising regularly
- Support healing of leaky gut and intestinal lining
- Reduce inflammation throughout the entire body
- Help restore optimal cortisol levels and healthy adrenal stress response
- Reduce exposure to toxins and pesticides
- Stabilize blood sugar levels

It can also:

- Aid in weight loss
- Help balance hormones
- Help improve sleep
- Be an effective overall detoxification program
- Help "reset" your body when you've been feeling unwell for a long time.

What symptoms can the Stress Remedy Program help alleviate?

The symptoms of leaky gut vary from person to person. The Stress Remedy Program can help alleviate many of the most common symptoms, such as:

- Chronic or frequent fatigue
- Chronic pain – muscle aches, frequent headaches, joint pain, etc.
- Sleep problems – inability to fall or stay asleep at night
- Digestive issues – bloating, reflux, IBS, discomfort
- Weight gain and difficulty losing weight
- Blood sugar imbalances
- Hormone imbalances
- Frequent skin rashes or allergic reactions

- Chronic infections – lungs, bladder, skin, sinus, vaginal, etc.
- Mood swings, anxiety, brain fog, etc.

What's included in the program?

Dr. Doni's Stress Remedy Program consists of:

- Guidebook with 51 gluten-free, dairy-free recipes and meal plan
- Daily email tips to help guide you during the program
- Access to a private Facebook group, so you can interact with others on the program

Optionally, you may purchase the following products to go with the program:

- **Pea Protein Shake:**

https://www.drdonistore.com/Dr-Donis-Pea-Protein-Shake_p_733.html

- **Leaky Gut Support:**

https://www.drdonistore.com/Dr-Donis-Leaky-Gut-Support-61-oz_p_681.html

- **Enzyme Support:**

https://www.drdonistore.com/-Dr-Donis-Enzyme-Support-90-capsules_p_977.html

- **Probiotic Support:**

https://www.drdonistore.com/Dr-Donis-Probiotic-Support-60-vegetarian-capsules_p_271.html

Is this the right program for me?

The Stress Remedy Program is most suitable for people who:

- Have leaky gut OR suspect they might have it
- Want support to change their diet and implement self care strategies
- Want to try out a clean eating program to see if it helps alleviate their symptoms
- Feel confident about doing a health optimizing program on their own
- May not be ready to work one-to-one with a naturopathic doctor

What if I want more help?

For those who desire a more personalized and comprehensive approach, Dr. Doni also offers a comprehensive one-on-one health consultation programs including a Sleep Solutions Program and Leaky Gut & Digestive Solutions Program. These consultation packages include recommended health panels, consultations with Dr. Doni, a private Facebook group and discounts on supplements.

Dr. Doni's Natural Sleep Solutions Program

Who is this for?

Dr. Doni's Natural Sleep Solutions Program package is for you if your life is negatively affected because you cannot fall asleep and/ or stay asleep at night and you'd like one-on-one help to identify solutions to correct the situation.

Dr. Doni has been helping people recover from sleep issues for over 18 years. She's developed a proven system to specifically address sleep issues. She knows what works and will show you exactly what to do.

The aims of this program are to:

- Identify the underlying cause of your sleep issues, through carefully-selected tests.

- Address the real reasons why you cannot sleep, so you can take control of your health.

- Show you which nutrients your body needs to address your sleep problems.

191

- Design a strategic plan that will reduce or eliminate your symptoms and restore your quality of life.

- Develop a long-term health plan to help you maintain high-quality sleep, which can also be instrumental in helping SOLVE a range of other underlying health issues, and make your overall life happier and healthier.

What is included in this program?

- You will have FIVE private consultations with Dr. Doni, spread out over a six-month period. These include:

- ONE comprehensive 60-minute consultation to discuss your health issues and individualize your sleep solutions plan.

- ONE extended 45-minute consultation to go through the results of your health panels, discuss progress and give recommendations.

- TWO regular 30-minute consultations to assess progress and make any necessary adjustments to your regimen.

- ONE brief 15-minute consultation to create an ongoing maintenance plan.

Patients are responsible for scheduling all consultations and follow-ups either via email or online. We recommend scheduling well in advance to ensure availability at your preferred time.

KINDLY NOTE: All consultations must be completed within the agreed 6 months. Additional consultations may be added as needed.

HEALTH PANELS

In this package, the following panels are included*:

- 4-timed cortisol panel
- Melatonin level
- Urinary neurotransmitter panel (serotonin, GABA, adrenaline, etc.)
- IgG and IgA food sensitivities panel for 96 foods

Some additional blood work may also be required (e.g. HgbA1c, thyroid, etc.), which can be done either through your doctor or through Dr. Doni's office.

ADDITIONAL SUPPORT

You will have access to a private Facebook group, where you can ask questions (and get answers!) about your health issues and treatment program, share experiences with other patients, and take advantage of special offers on health supplements, available only to members of the group.

SUPPLEMENTS and NUTRIENTS

While this package does not include supplements, it en titles you to a 10% discount on ANY supplements you purchase from DRDONISTORE.COM for 6 months.

EXTRAS INCLUDED

As part of your program, you will also receive:

- A summarized list of foods for you to avoid, based on your results

- A paperback copy of Dr. Doni's book The Stress Remedy (retail value $25)

- The Stress Remedy 21-Day Program including daily email tips, meal plan and recipes to support you with any diet and health changes you make during your program (retail value $97)

How do I get started?

Reach out to us at
office@doctordoni.com

and

DoctorDoni.com
to request an appointment to work with Dr. Doni.

ABOUT DR. DONI WILSON,
NATUROPATHIC DOCTOR

DR. **DONI WILSON, N.D.** is a Doctor of Naturopathic Medicine, natural health expert, nutritionist and midwife. She specializes in gluten sensitivity, intestinal permeability, adrenal stress, insulin resistance, neurotransmitter imbalances, hypothyroidism, women's health issues, autoimmunity and genetic variations called "SNPs," which can have a profound impact upon your health.

For nearly 20 years, she has helped women, men and children overcome their most perplexing health challenges and achieve their wellness goals by crafting individualized strategies that address the whole body and the underlying causes of health issues.

DR. DONI is the creator of The Stress Remedy Programs and author of *The Stress Remedy: Master Your Body's Synergy*

& Optimize Your Health as well as the #1 bestselling books *Stress Remedies: How to Reduce Stress and Boost Your Health in Just 15 Minutes a Day and Stress Warrior.*

Professional affiliations...

- American Association of Naturopathic Physicians (past board member)

- New York Association of Naturopathic Physicians (president and executive director 2003 – 2013)

- American Association of Naturopathic Midwives (past board member)

- Connecticut Naturopathic Physicians Association

- Endocrinology Association of Naturopathic Physicians

- Pediatric Association of Naturopathic Physicians

- Association for the Advancement of Restorative Medicine

Dr. Doni's research and approach to health optimization has been featured on TV, radio, podcasts, and print, including GOOP, Natural Solutions Magazine, First for Women Magazine, Huffington Post, Elle Magazine, Inspiyr Magazine, Mind Body Green, Energy Times, Fox News, and more. She publishes a blog and podcast at DoctorDoni.com, and is the owner of Nature Empowered Nutritionals and Cat Care, a not-for-profit dedicated to animal rights.

Made in the USA
Middletown, DE
28 May 2020